Roman Republic

An Enthralling Overview of the Rise and Fall

Free limited time bonus

Stop for a moment. We have a free bonus set up for you. The problem is this: we forget 90% of everything that we read after 7 days. Crazy fact, right? Here's the solution: we've created a printable, 1-page pdf summary for this book that you're reading now. All you have to do to get your free pdf summary is to go to the following website: **https://livetolearn.lpages.co/enthrallinghistory/**

Once you do, it will be intuitive. Enjoy, and thank you!

We forget 90% of everything that we've read in 7 days...

Get the free printable pdf summary of the book you've read AND much, much more... shhhh...

Enter Your Most Frequently Used Email to Get Started

DOWNLOAD FREE PDF SUMMARY

© Enthralling History

Table of Contents

Introduction

In the dead of night, Prince Tarquin crept through the house, silently stepping over the bodyguard sleeping at Lucretia's door. He gently opened the door and slipped in. There! In the moonlight shining through the window, he saw the exquisite woman deep in sleep. He had met her earlier when he was a guest of her husband Collatinus, who often expressed pride in his cherished wife's stunning looks and exemplary character. One look and Tarquin was desperate to have her.

Stealthily, he approached her bed and placed his hand over her mouth as Lucretia awoke with a start. "Shh! It's me, Prince Tarquin. Oh, beautiful Lucretia! I have thought of nothing else since I first saw you. I want you for my own! Marry me, and be my queen. We will rule Rome together!"

Lucretia desperately struggled to push Tarquin away, but pressing his sword to her belly, he hissed, "Give in! Otherwise, I'll kill you and your bodyguard. I'll say I found him sleeping with you! What will your husband think of your virtue then?"

In the morning, Lucretia dressed in black and messaged her father and husband, who were with the army, laying siege on Ardea. "Come at once! Bring two witnesses with you."

Lucretia told her husband, father, and their two friends what Tarquin had done to her. The men comforted and reassured her, saying, "You did not consent, so you have no guilt; you have not sinned!"

But the distraught Lucretia cried out, "Give me your oath! Avenge my rape!"

She slipped a dagger from under her pillow and plunged it into her heart as Collatinus screamed in horror. Sobbing and shattered, he clasped her to him, kissing her and stroking her hair. "Lucretia! My darling wife! Oh, my poor Lucretia."

Her father and the other men collapsed to the floor, wailing. But then Brutus, one of the witnesses, suddenly stood up, jerked the dagger out of Lucretia's breast, and held it up, her blood dripping down his arm. "By Mars and all the gods, I will overthrow the power of the evil Tarquinii clan! We've had enough of tyrants ruling over us! We cannot tolerate this any longer. With Lucretia's blood, I swear my oath! Who is with me?"

Each man reached for the dagger, swearing, "By Lucretia's pure blood, we shall avenge this outrage by the king's son. The gods are our witnesses! We will drive out King Lucius Tarquinius Superbus, his accursed wife, and all his family! By fire, sword, and every means possible, we will eradicate the reign of kings over Rome!"[1]

Thus ended the Roman monarchy. It would soon be replaced by the Roman Republic. After tyrannical kings abused their power, the Romans boldly established a form of government never seen before, one that would influence new governments two millennia later. In its metamorphosis from a modest city-state, Rome conquered and ruled vast territories around the Mediterranean. The Romans were master assimilators, putting new knowledge and techniques into play in their evolving political system. And yet, social unrest, economic crises, and political instability rocked the republic until it eventually crumbled after five centuries.

We have much to learn from the sensational rise and cataclysmic fall of the Roman Republic. This book will bring the remarkable men and women who formed the republic to life as we examine how their brilliant triumphs and asinine misjudgments unfolded. What were the distinctive pillars of the republic's nascent government? How did the Romans ascend to power over central Italy only to be crushed by the Celts? Like a phoenix rising from the

---

[1] Titus Livius, *The History of Rome, Vol. 1*, trans. George Baker (New York: Peter A. Mesier et al., 10). https://oll.libertyfund.org/title/baker-the-history-of-rome-vol-1.

ashes, how did they bounce back, more competent and cunning, to confront Pyrrhus's war elephants in the Pyrrhic Wars and crush Carthage in the Punic Wars? As Rome warred with Greece, what factors led to supremacy over the Achaean League and Macedonia?

And how did it all come crashing down? What social inequalities led to Rome's civil wars and internal storms? How did Spartacus's great slave revolt unfold? Why did the republican government unravel so much that Caesar, Pompey, and Crassus sidestepped the constitutional checks and balances, forming the First Triumvirate? How did Julius Caesar manipulate events to become Rome's dictator for life, and why did a mob of senators stab him to death?

Many books have been written about Rome, but this overview of the Roman Republic is not simply a chronological assortment of dry facts. It explores the enthralling stories of real people in all their pride and passion: the foresighted fathers of Rome's constitution, the ingenious military leaders, the disenfranchised lower classes, and the nefarious plotters. They all made Rome what it was for an astounding five centuries of empire-building, intrigue, and brutal feuds.

Exploring history is incredibly advantageous, as it helps us understand how our world got to where we are. In the past five centuries, over a hundred countries have abandoned monarchies or empires to form a government modeled on the founding principles of the Roman Republic. Understanding the past in all its glory and chaotic destruction inspires, instructs, and cautions us. What can Rome's experience teach us about today's social, economic, and political struggles? Let's step back twenty-seven centuries and find out.

PART ONE: Life and Times of the Early Republic (500 BCE)

Chapter 1: The Early Republic

How was Rome ruled before it became a republic? For over two centuries, kings ruled Rome, some exemplary and some inept. The last king, Tarquinius Superbus (known as Tarquin), was evil personified. To comprehend his diabolical depths, we must step back a generation to Servius Tullius, the previous king. Tullius was the son of a slave-woman, and no one was sure who his father was, but whispers swirled that he was King Tarquinius Priscus's illegitimate son.

One night, screams rang out from the palace as assassins snuck in and murdered King Tarquinius. His sons were too young to rule, and Queen Tanaquil knew the Senate would elect another man to the throne. She had to make a quick decision to hold on to power so one of her sons could have a chance to rule. So, she plotted with Tullius.

Hurrying out to the balcony, she called down to the crowd assembled below, "The king is alive! He is seriously injured, but he is recovering from the attack. In the meantime, he has assigned Tullius to take care of his affairs."

For several weeks, Tullius pretended to be acting on orders from the king as the royal guard hunted down the assassins and executed some, while others fled the country. Then, Tanaquil walked out on the balcony again. "My dearest people, I bring sad news. My husband has died of his wounds. He assigned Tullius as his regent until our sons are old enough to rule."[2]

Tullius became the de facto king while the boys were growing up, but even when they came of age, he kept the throne. Through those years, he cultivated popularity with the working-class plebeians by giving them land. Only landowners could vote, and, of course, they would vote for him. He even initiated a plan to emancipate the enslaved people and grant them citizenship. He infuriated the patrician aristocrats, who didn't want to lose their slaves.

Tullius assured Tanaquil's sons he would relinquish the throne when the time was right and gave his two daughters in marriage to the two princes. But the oldest son, Tarquin, knew he would never be king as long as Tullius lived. After his younger brother Arruns refused to join him in a coup, Tarquin angrily conspired with his brother's wife, Tullia Minor, and they poisoned Arruns. When Tarquin's wife criticized his devilry, he poisoned her, then married her sister, Tullia Minor.

Tarquin had been stirring up the senators and patricians, who disliked the king's support of the oppressed commoners and slaves. Hearing that Tarquin was in the Senate denouncing his kingship, King Tullius rushed to the building. But Tarquin grabbed him by his toga and pushed him out of the building, sending him tumbling down the steps. Tullius sat, bruised and confused, on the pavement, wondering why no one came to his aid. And where did his bodyguards get off to?

As Tullius limped away to be murdered by Tarquin's henchmen, the Senate elected Tarquin as Rome's new king. Hearing the news, his wife Tullia (Tullius's daughter) rushed to the Senate to congratulate her husband, then jumped back into her chariot. Charging full speed down the cobblestones, she ran over her father's body. The new king (and the last) protected himself against assassins by keeping a wall of bodyguards around him. He eliminated all the senators who might challenge him by executing or banishing most on trumped-up charges and clandestinely murdering others.[3]

---

[2] Cassius Dio, *Roman History*, trans. H. B. Foster (Vol. I, Loeb Classical Library edition, New York: Macmillan Publishers, 1914).
https://penelope.uchicago.edu/Thayer/E/Roman/Texts/Cassius_Dio/1*.html.

[3] Livius, *The History of Rome, Vol. 1*.

Tullia drove over her father's body. Painting by Jean Bardin.
https://commons.wikimedia.org/wiki/File:Bardin_Tullia.jpg

Tarquin didn't even trust his close friends who had supported his coup d'état. Instead of appointing them as senators, he suppressed the Senate's power. He ruled with only his sons, paranoid that anyone else would kill or displace him. He even killed family members he considered a threat, including his sister's son and husband. Her other son, Brutus, pretended to be mentally impaired, so Tarquin left him alone.

Brutus spearheaded the revolution after Lucretia's rape, toppling his uncle's throne and ending the monarchy begun by the wolf-child Romulus, Rome's mythical founder. A crowd gathered as the men carried Lucretia's body into the Forum. Brutus explained that he wasn't really mentally disabled; it was a ruse to survive King Tarquin's purges. Now he called out, "Act like men and Romans! Take up arms against our shameless enemies!"

One look at Lucretia's bloodstained corpse convinced most of the crowd. The senators knew a change was necessary for their survival. King Tarquin and his sons had ruled through fear and coercion and were hated by most Romans. With the crowd's approval, the senators voted to end the monarchy, eject the Tarquin family, and establish a different type of government. The royal family slipped out of Rome, away from the angry citizens, to drum up support from a few Etruscan and Latin cities.

In 509 BCE, Rome's citizens created a new government: the republic. They annually elected magistrates, established assemblies representing the people, and instituted the separation of powers. The stronger constitution required checks and balances to keep politicians in line. Politics now included novel concepts like filibusters, impeachments, quorum requirements, regular elections, term limits, and vetoes. The constitution was fluid, driven by Rome's expanding borders and tensions between the plebeian workers and the patrician aristocrats.

Instead of a king, the new republic established two heads of state called consuls, who ruled jointly for a one-year term. The first two consuls were Lucius Junius Brutus, the ringleader of the revolution, and Lucius Tarquinius Collatinus, Lucretia's husband. They immediately appointed new senators, bringing the number back to three hundred. Oddly, the consuls were both members of the Tarquin family that had been forced into exile. Brutus was King Tarquinius Superbus's nephew and King Tarquinius Priscus's grandson. Collatinus was King Tarquinius Priscus's nephew and a first cousin of his wife's rapist, Prince Tarquin.

Within weeks, the Tarquinian conspiracy arose: the exiled king's attempt to recapture his throne. He still had insiders among Rome's elite stirring up dissent. Brutus was unaware that his two sons and his wife's brothers were the chief conspirators. A slave named Vindicius came upon a gruesome scene. The plotters were gathered around the corpse of a man they'd killed, swearing an oath by pouring out his blood and touching his intestines. Unnoticed, Vindicius slipped away to tell the consuls that the conspirators had sworn to kill them. Soldiers arrested the rebels and discovered letters to King Tarquin in their possession.

Brutus sentenced his own sons to death for conspiracy.

Painting by Heinrich Friedrich Fuger. Photo modified: zoomed in. © José Luiz Bernardes Ribeiro;
https://commons.wikimedia.org/wiki/File:Brutus_Sentences_his_Sons_to_Death_by_Heinrich_Friedr
ich_Fuger_-_Staatsgalerie_-_Stuttgart_-_Germany_2017.jpg

Brutus sentenced his sons, Titus and Tiberius, to death, grimly watching their execution. After the rest of the conspirators were executed, the Romans were uneasy about Collatinus; after all, he was a Tarquin. Collatinus resigned as consul and went into exile. Brutus's execution of his sons spared his removal.[4] Yet before his one-year term was up, he died in battle against the former royal family. He and his first cousin, Prince Arruns, impaled each other in a cavalry charge.

The center of the new republic was the Forum: Rome's political, religious, and social hub. Initially a rectangular open-air gathering place, it soon housed elegant arches, basilicas, monuments, statues, and temples. People assembled in the Forum for business affairs, criminal trials, elections, gladiator matches, public meetings, religious ceremonies, speeches, and trade. The Senate met in the Forum to debate proposed laws and vote.

---

[4] Plutarch, *The Parallel Lives.* (Volume I: Loeb Classical Library edition, 1914).
https://penelope.uchicago.edu/hayer/E/Roman/Texts/Plutarch/Lives/Publicola*.html.

From its inception, constant warfare defined the Roman Republic. For the first two hundred years, Rome warred against other Italian tribes and the invading Celts. The Romans displayed incredible tenacity in heroic battles and sprang back from catastrophic losses. From 483 to 476 BCE, Rome fended off the Etruscan city of Veii, just ten miles north of Rome. The Etruscans allied with the Sabines, an Apennine Mountain tribe. After joining the nearby Latins, their kinsmen, the Romans finally defeated the Veientes and Sabines, forcing them to pay tribute.

In 458 BCE, another Apennine Mountain tribe called the Aequi attacked while Rome was dealing with a slave revolt, the death of a consul, and friction between the plebeians and patricians. Rome defeated the Aequi, but the following year, the Aequi appeared again, to the Romans' great annoyance. In a time of great peril, the Roman constitution permitted the Romans to nominate a temporary dictator to deal with the crisis, and they chose Cincinnatus. The brilliant leader defeated the Aequi in sixteen days with hardly any bloodshed. He then resigned from his dictatorship and returned to his farm.

Suddenly, a new enemy exploded onto the scene: the Celts from eastern Gaul (France). The Gallic Senones had surged over the Alps, wreaking havoc in northern Italy and then settling down and building Mediolanum (today's Milan). Hearing of central Italy's rich farmland that produced olives, figs, and grapes for fine wines, the Senones sent their warriors to invade the Etruscan city of Clusium. When the Etruscans appealed to Rome for help, the Romans sent three ambassadors, who informed the Celts that if they attacked Clusium, they would have to fight Rome.

The tense standoff ended in a brawl, and one of the ambassadors killed a Senone war chief, a grave breach of the ancient law shared by the nations. Rome was unprepared for the consequences. With lightning speed, the Senones, led by their chieftain Brennus, marched out to confront Rome. The Romans quickly mustered their army and met the Senones at the Tiber River, several miles north of Rome.

In the 390 BCE Battle of the Allia, the Senone chief Brennus charged through the Romans' middle line, cutting its army in two. In terror, Rome's left flank plunged into the river, where many drowned, weighed down by their armor in the swift current. The ones who managed to swim to the other side escaped to Veii. Meanwhile, the right flank desperately made a break for Rome; over half the Roman army fell in battle or drowned that day.

The Senones couldn't believe they had so easily trounced Rome. They set about pillaging the Roman camp for two days, then arrived at Rome at sunset. Oddly, the city gates were open, and no one appeared to be defending the city. Was it a trap? The Celts decided to wait until morning, unwilling to walk into an ambush at night. The gates were, in fact, undefended. Most of the Romans had fled to the hills. The army and the city leaders had fenced off the steep Capitoline Hill inside Rome and were bunkered down at the top. Some elderly priests and former consuls arrayed themselves in their finest robes and sat in their ivory chairs in the Forum.

In the morning, the Celts hesitantly entered Rome, expecting an attack at any moment. But no one challenged them. It was a ghost town! Making their way to the Forum, they found the elders stoically seated in majestic splendor. Were they gods? One Celt reached out to touch an ancient patrician's beard and received a rap on the head with the elder's staff. They were men! The invaders hewed down the elders and anyone else foolish enough to stay in the city, but the men on the steep Capitoline Hill behind the barricades managed to hold them off.

The death of the Consul Papirius by Philipp Friedrich Hetsch.
https://commons.wikimedia.org/wiki/File:The_Death_of_the_Consul_Papirius,_by_Philipp_Friedrich_Hetsch,_1795,_oil_on_canvas_-_Germanisches_Nationalmuseum_-_Nuremberg,_Germany_-_DSC03431.jpg

The rest of Rome was wide open for the Celts to plunder and burn, which they did so for the next seven months, destroying relics and records of Rome's ancient history. The military on Capitoline Hill had stockpiled food, but the Senones were scavenging the surrounding farms and villages. The one-time Roman dictator Camillus, who had been exiled by political enemies, lived in the town of Ardea. He and the men of Ardea observed that the Celts got drunk at night, so they launched a night raid, wiping out the raiding party. This victory motivated the Roman soldiers in Veii to ask Camillus to lead them in retaking Rome.

Camillus agreed but insisted that Rome's leadership had to reverse his exile and officially endorse his new dictatorship. For that to happen, someone had to communicate with the Roman leaders bunkered down at Capitoline Hill. A young man knew of a secret path up the hill, so he snuck into Rome by night, climbing up the steep cliffside. He met with the senators, who appointed Camillus as dictator. Camillus put together an army of twelve thousand men, including Etruscan allies. At this point, the men on Capitoline Hill were starving. How long would it be before Camillus's force could rescue them?[5]

The Celts were likewise suffering from dysentery in a city reeking of rotting, unburied corpses in the summer heat. The Senones were hill people with no acquired immunity to malaria, which devastated their numbers. Chief Brennus met with Rome's tribune Sulpicius to mediate an end to the siege. The Celts agreed to leave Rome in exchange for one thousand pounds of gold. But the Romans felt the scale was faulty. As the Senones and Romans were contesting the scale's integrity, Camillus suddenly marched in with his twelve thousand soldiers. Pointing his sword at the Celts, he snarled, "Leave now, Senones! Iron will deliver Rome, not gold!"[6]

The Senones only retreated eight miles from Rome, which proved to be fatal. Camillus attacked the next day, annihilating the entire Celtic army. Rome spent the next fifty years rebuilding the city and consolidating authority over the central and southern Italian tribes. By 295 BCE, Rome ruled over all of central Italy and most

---

[5] Livius, *The History of Rome, Vol. 3.*
[6] Plutarch, *The Parallel Lives, Vol. 2.*

of the southern peninsula. Now, it was time to conquer the Mediterranean.

The Pyrrhic War, which lasted from 280 to 275 BCE, involved Epirus "aiding" the Greek city-states of southern Italy in their struggle against Rome. Sicily, Carthage, and Italy's Samnite and Etruscan tribes all got involved in battles, which ultimately brought southern Italy under the Roman fold. Then, Rome and Carthage clashed in the legendary Punic Wars, which lasted from 264 to 146 BCE, while Rome simultaneously fought against the Macedonian Kingdom, the Achaean League in Corinth, and the Seleucid Empire.

Rome's most lethal war was its toxic conflict between the working-class plebeians and the aristocratic patricians. The plebeians lost their ancestral farmland to huge slave-operated plantations owned by the patricians, who grew fabulously wealthy as the plebeians sunk deeper into debt. A group of prisoner-of-war slaves led a revolt, amassing an army of thousands. They were able to hold off the Roman forces at Mount Vesuvius.

Rome's internal unrest led to the First Triumvirate, led by Crassus, Rome's richest man, and two brilliant war heroes: Pompey and Caesar. This leadership change spelled the beginning of the end for the Roman Republic. It opened the door to the Roman Empire, which would be led by emperors instead of consuls. Throughout the five centuries of the republic, the Romans had to adapt to several challenges. They evolved from a city-state into a republic that spanned three continents, stretching from the Middle East to Britain and south to North Africa.

How would the conquered territories be ruled, though? The elite Romans had to deal with the plebeian commoners, who demanded equal representation in the government, and the question of freeing the slaves. No sooner was one predicament addressed than another emerged. But they weathered the crises for five centuries while conquering 750,000 square miles of territory and spreading their language, culture, and political system throughout the known world.

Chapter 2: Politics and Political Influence

What did this new government of the Roman Republic look like? Its official title was *Senatus Populusque Romanus*: the Senate and People of Rome. After perceiving that rule by hereditary kingship was rife with problems, the Romans established a government that endured until 27 BCE, when emperors began ruling Rome. Up to this point, most nations were monarchies, except for Greece, where Athens was developing a democracy. A republic was a completely new system. It did not have a king, but it was not quite a democracy either, especially not in the beginning. Athenian democracy was a government where all classes had a vote, while the elite patricians initially held power in the Roman Republic.

When Rome was a city-state, its legal system applied only to Roman citizens: male descendants of Rome's founding tribes. As it began to conquer neighboring regions, the new territories' courts decided on legal disputes based on their own laws. However, as Rome expanded and conquered other nations, they used the *jus gentium* or "law of nations" for non-Romans living within new Roman territory. These were basic "natural" laws and legal traditions that most nations of the day considered universal.

As for Rome itself, the republic started with unwritten laws based on customs and precedents. The Twelve Tables, which stood in the Forum, was Rome's first written legislation, passed in 450 BCE to provide a standard code for all citizens. Before this, the plebeian working class often had no idea what the laws were, leaving them vulnerable to abuse by the patrician upper class. The Twelve Tables consolidated earlier unwritten laws on legal procedures, family laws, property laws, personal injury laws, and sacred laws.

Rome's constitution was a work in process. Its earliest rules were unwritten, such as laws dealing with elections, assemblies, and Senate functions. Later, new legislation inscribed in bronze was placed at eye level in public areas where all could read them. Of course, not everyone could read, but they were available so literate individuals could explain them to the masses. The Senate issued new decrees by recommending a course of action for the magistrates to enforce.[7] An innovation of the Romans was the power of *intercessio* or veto. A consul could veto his co-consul's actions, and tribunes could protect the plebeians by vetoing senatorial decrees.

Each year, two men were elected to serve as consuls. In Rome, the consuls were the chief administrators of all aspects of life, with all other leaders subordinate to them except for the tribunes. They decided what business the Senate would discuss and enforced the Senate's mandates. They also were the commanders in chief of the military.[8] Rome often had two forces fighting on different fronts, so the consuls would split up. For instance, one might be fighting in Greece, while the other would be in Carthage.

Why two commanders in chief? Some city-states already had two kings, such as in Sparta, where one headed the military and the other the political arena. But the kings usually served for life, while Rome's consuls served for one year. For the Romans, it was a matter of checks and balances; if one consul made idiotic decisions, the other could veto him. If a consul abused his powers, he faced prosecution at the end of his term. One consul led the Centuriate Assembly, which was comprised of military centuries (one hundred soldiers); each century's collective vote was counted rather than individual votes. The other consul led the Assembly of Tribes, a non-military assembly where each "tribe" represented a

---

[7] Andrew Lintott, *The Constitution of the Roman Republic* (Oxford: Oxford University Press, 2003), 1-4.

[8] Lintott, *The Constitution*, 17.

geographical division.

The Roman monarchy had senators whose chief function was to elect kings and advise them. The senators' role changed in the Roman Republic. They instead gave "recommendations" to the magistrates, who essentially considered them new laws. In the monarchy, the Senate had focused on internal affairs; in the republic, the senators concentrated on foreign policy for all the new regions Rome was conquering. They controlled the budget, giving them power over the military. Senatorial power over all aspects of the Roman Republic grew over time.

In the early republic, the consuls appointed senators from the elite patrician class. After about two centuries, new senators were appointed for a life term out of a pool of magistrates, including plebeians and freed slaves. The republic started out with one hundred senators but grew to three hundred by 312 BCE. Some consuls liked to "pack" the Senate with appointees who were likely to support them, so by the end of the Roman Republic, the number of senators grew to one thousand.

If Rome was embroiled in a crisis, the Senate could recommend a temporary dictator. One of the consuls would nominate him to the *Comitia Curiata* (the Curiate Assembly) for approval. The dictator only served for the length of the crisis, which would last anywhere from several weeks to a few months. After the first three centuries of the republic, the plebeians' power over the position of dictator drastically weakened it.

Censors and praetors served under the consuls. The censors administered the census and "censored" what they considered public immorality or a breach of ethics. They had the power to strip a person of citizenship if he committed unworthy actions.[9] The praetors served dual roles as army generals and judges. When Rome's borders extended out of Italy, the praetors became governors of the provinces. If both consuls were away at war, the *praetor urbanus* led Rome.

Living in Rome didn't automatically make a person a citizen. Only non-enslaved males aged sixteen and up who descended from Rome's original tribes could be full citizens. Women could have

---

[9] Livius, *The History of Rome*, Vol. 4.

limited citizenship through their fathers or husbands but could not vote, hold political office, or attend assemblies. To flaunt their status, citizens wore white togas, the symbol of full legal rights, including voting rights. Citizens belonged to the Curate Assembly (*Comitia Curiata*), where they cast their votes on legislative matters. The Curate Assembly was later split into the Assembly of Tribes and the Centuriate Assembly. A third assembly, the Plebeian Assembly, was added in 494 BCE to represent the working class.

Two other political roles were tribunes and magistrates. With up to ten elected tribunes, the *tribunus plebis* led the Plebeian Assembly for the working class. They proposed legislation for the assembly's vote and vetoed senatorial legislation that favored the aristocrats over the ordinary people. The military tribunes held a high rank in the army and served at least five years. Each legion, which consisted of about five thousand men, had two commanders serving from a rotation of six tribunes. The *tribuni aerarii* administered the treasury and tax collection. The tribuni militum consulari potestate (military tribunes with consular authority) occasionally served instead of consuls in the early republic. A plebeian could be a military tribune with consular authority but not a consul.

Magistrates had authority over a specific geographical area or a particular duty. The patricians and eventually the plebeians elected them for one-year terms. After their year was up, they couldn't stand for election for another decade. The two top magistrates were the consuls, and if the times called for a dictator, he would be a magistrate. Other magistrates served as military commanders, censors, praetors, and tribunes.

At the top of Rome's society and politics were the patricians: wealthy, aristocratic citizens from fifty leading families (*gens*) with large farms. Among the most prominent ancient families were the Cornelii, Claudii, Fabii, Valerii, and Aemilii. Most of the population was in the middle and formed the plebeian working class. The enslaved people were at the bottom of society; these people were prisoners of war or people enslaved due to their debts. The enslaved population comprised up to 20 percent of Rome's population and had virtually no rights.

Initially, the patricians held almost absolute power over the government, religious affairs, and the military. They served as patrons for "clients," usually plebeians and freed slaves (freedmen) considered part of the extended *gens* (family clan). The patrons negotiated marriages and provided food, legal assistance, protection, financial loans, and assistance with business transactions. The clients would greet their patron at dawn with their needs, and after assisting them, the patron would walk to the Forum, accompanied by his clients. The more clients he had, the higher his prestige!

The plebeians (plebs) were the working class. They were the bakers, builders, craftsmen, farmers, and small business owners, to name a few. In the early republic, they held minimal political clout, but that quickly changed, as they realized the patricians depended on them for life's basic needs. In the Conflict of the Orders—the struggle of the plebeians against patrician discrimination—they exercised *secessio plebis*: "plebeian withdrawal" or going on strike. They left their shops, farms, and even the army for a short time. The patricians had to fend for themselves. The strike reminded them how much they depended on the plebeians and forced them to listen to the plebeians' grievances.

The plebeian soldiers refused to fight due to injustices. Artist: B. Barloccini.
https://commons.wikimedia.org/wiki/File:Secessio_plebis.JPG

One injustice at the top of the plebeians' list was the senators failing to inform the plebeians of new laws, which resulted in the magistrates arresting them for breaking them. The plebeians were fined or imprisoned for laws they didn't even know existed. Another grievance for the plebeians was losing the lands where they had been tenant farmers, as the aristocratic landowners began using more slave labor due to all the prisoners of war.

All the plebeians could do was head to the towns and cities and try to find work. They would endure beatings and imprisonment if they couldn't pay their debts. Gradually, the plebeians began to win political leverage with their strikes. In 494 BCE, the plebeian soldiers went on strike when Rome clashed with the Aequi, Sabines, and Volsci. Their refusal to fight the enemy won them the Plebeian Council, the plebeian tribune, and the right to vote for their officials.

After Rome conquered the Hernici tribe south of Rome in 486 BCE, the consul Spurius Cassius Vecellinus proposed giving one-third of the Hernici lands to the plebeians. Another one-third would go to their Latin allies who had helped win the war, and the Hernici would keep one-third of their farms. The patricians hated this idea because they wouldn't get any land. They saw Cassius as a traitor. He was tried for treason and executed at the end of his one-year term.

When the Senone Gauls sacked Rome, the plebeians suffered devastating losses to their shops and farms. The military also suffered, as the men weren't paid for their services and had no income from their destroyed shops, farms, or trades. Marcus Manlius Capitolinus, a former consul and war hero, saw a centurion he knew who had defended Rome. The centurion was now poverty-stricken, unable to pay his debts. When Manlius saw him marched to prison, he jumped in and paid his debt on the spot.

After this experience, Manlius became increasingly aware of the crushing debt looming over most of the plebeians and did what he could to help them. He sold his land to pay off debts and advocated on their behalf against the Senate, which was misusing funds that could ease the plebeians' suffering. His efforts at swaying the Senate did not go well; the patricians pushed him off the eighty-foot-high Tarpeian Rock, killing him.

However, Camillus, who had earlier obliterated the Senones, was appointed dictator again to fight another Celtic onslaught. He surprisingly came to the plebeians' aid after initially siding with the patricians. The plebeians demanded one of the consuls be plebeian, and Camillus negotiated an agreement with the Senate. He built the Temple of Concord next to the Forum to celebrate the new co-rule of plebeians and patricians.

Soon, the plebeians began filling the offices of censor and dictator, but as they progressed in political status, some became nouveau-riche social climbers. The new elites were excited about their surge to the top while ignoring the needs of the working poor. However, the brothers Tiberius and Gaius Gracchus, who both served as plebeian tribunes, championed social reform yet paid a bitter price.

The Gracchi brothers advocated for land redistribution.
Jean-Baptiste Claude Eugène Guillaume;
https://commons.wikimedia.org/wiki/File:Eugene_Guillaume_-_the_Gracchi.jpg

As Rome conquered additional territory, the aristocratic patricians grabbed most of the newly acquired farmland. After Tiberius's election in 133 BCE, he proposed that the maximum property one person could hold should be about 325 acres. The rest of the land would be redistributed to the war veterans and homeless poor in plots of about twenty acres. The senators hated the idea because they would have to give up a lot of lands, which were their source of wealth.

Tiberius's term was running out, and the matter was still unsettled, so he ran for reelection. But running for a consecutive term went against precedent. His political enemies accused him of aspiring to be a tyrant (an absolute ruler who comes into power outside the usual channels). On election day, the senators and other patricians led a mob that surrounded Tiberius and three hundred supporters, beating them to death with wooden chairs and clubs.

Tiberius's brother Gaius was elected as tribune ten years later. He supported his brother's land redistribution reform and insisted on the government funding basic armor and weapons for the soldiers. Many poor citizens were drafted into the military but went into debt paying for their equipment. His political opponents stirred up a riot, and one of the rioters died in the fray, stirring the Senate to declare Gaius an enemy of the state without a jury trial. Gaius committed suicide before he could be executed, but the Senate rounded up three thousand of his supporters and executed them.

The plebeian tribune Drusus continued to fight for land redistribution and for everyone living in Italy to become citizens. His assassination sparked the Social War (91–87 BCE), as the Italian tribes revolted, demanding the right to vote in Rome's elections and to be protected by Roman law. The Senate appointed Gaius Marius, a plebeian tribune and uncle to Julius Caesar, to subdue the rebels. As the war dragged on, Marius killed or captured thirteen thousand rebels but then became ill and had to end the campaign. Despite technically winning the brutal war, Rome finally gave citizenship rights and the right to vote to all free males on Italy's mainland.

Chapter 3: Societal Roles and Culture

Rome's extraordinary military conquests are enthralling to read about, as are its political intrigues, but what about the lives of the ordinary people? How did they live? What sort of jobs did they have? What did they eat, and what were their living conditions? What were their gender roles and expectations? And how did slavery impact Roman society? Let's explore

What sort of housing did the Romans have? It depended on the family's economic status. About 80 percent of the urban population lived in tiny apartments in buildings known as *insulae*. These multi-family dwellings could house up to fifty people and were three to five stories high. Some were higher, but after fires and earthquakes killed many citizens, laws limited the height of new buildings.

The first floor usually had shops, and the upper floors contained two-room apartments for families, although some *insulae* had larger apartments on the lower floors. The *insulae* surrounded a city block, with a row of connected rowhouses running along the street and a central courtyard in the middle. Most *insulae* were constructed of shoddy materials, such as wood and mudbrick, making them susceptible to fire and collapse.

This 3ʳᵈ-century BCE insula is west of Rome in Ostia.
https://commons.wikimedia.org/wiki/File:OstianInsulae.JPG

Wealthy aristocrats usually had two homes: a single-family *domus* in the city and a large private villa in the suburbs or the countryside. The *domus* had an exquisitely decorated entryway leading to the atrium, a grand hall where the hosts welcomed their guests. A large rectangular opening in the atrium's roof let in sunlight, and directly underneath was a shallow pool that collected rainwater with pipes leading to an underground cistern. The family left offerings to the household gods and their ancestral spirits at a household shrine in the atrium.

Rooms leading out of the atrium included the *tablinum* or the master's office, where the men received their clients' appeals and conducted business. The dining room was spectacularly decorated, with murals on the walls and tile mosaics on the floor to dazzle the family's frequent dinner-party guests. Instead of chairs, the dining room had several couches, where the family and guests reclined to eat from small tables. A garden often graced the rear of the home.

The villas of upper-class families didn't have the noise, offensive odors, and crime of the city and were a pleasant weekend retreat. Often, this was where the wife and children spent most of their time, as it was comfortable and offered more space for the children to play. Like the *domus*, they usually had a central, open-air atrium or courtyard surrounded by living areas, bedrooms, and servant quarters.

Exquisite frescoes like this one in Pompeii decorated Roman villas.
https://commons.wikimedia.org/wiki/File:Roman_fresco_Villa_dei_Misteri_Pompeii_001.jpg

Close to the time the Roman Republic was established, the Etruscans built Rome's first sewers. The Cloaca Maxima, which still operates today, was an open channel that drained the marshy areas, reducing the malaria-causing mosquitoes. It was later covered and used to drain rainwater from the streets and sewage from the public latrines into the Tiber River.[10] The *insulae* had running water on the lower floors but no indoor toilets. Everyone had to use a public latrine or chamber pots.

Daily life for people in the Roman Republic depended on one's social class and level of wealth. Rome's population wasn't just Roman. It never was just Roman, even in their mythological beginnings. When Romulus founded Rome, there weren't enough

---

[10] Emily Gowers, "The Anatomy of Rome from Capitol to Cloaca," *The Journal of Roman Studies* Vol.85 (1995): 23-32.

women for all the men, so they abducted young women from the Sabine tribe to marry. Further back in time, Romulus's ancestors were refugees from Troy who intermarried with the Latin tribe. Rome's founding families were a blend of several ethnicities.

Rome was a cosmopolitan mixture of Italian tribes and merchant traders from around the Mediterranean: Egyptians and Carthaginians from North Africa, Syrians and Jews from the Levant, and seafaring Greeks. As the republic conquered and expanded, Rome drew in people from present-day Spain, France, and Great Britain. The Roman military and merchants traveled and lived on three continents. That meant many Romans were multi-lingual and adopted some of the food, apparel, and customs from other parts of the world.

For all its grandeur, the streets of Rome could be unpleasant. Before indoor plumbing became widely available, chamber pots of feces and urine were emptied from windows and balconies to the street below, leaving a smelly, slippery, unhygienic mess for pedestrians to gingerly tread through. Rome was rife with crime, especially at night. And its population of at least a million was noisy.

What sort of medical assistance was available in a crowded, unsanitary city with the looming threat of malaria? Tomb art shows a woman giving birth in a unique reclining chair with an opening in the seat for the newborn to pass through. Artifacts show Roman doctors had steel forceps, probes, scalpels, and wound retractors. Most doctors in Rome were Greek and believed the Greek god Apollo and other Greek deities had healing powers. When a plague swept through Italy in 431 BCE, they built a temple to Apollo Medicus in Rome. Romans who didn't use Greek doctors depended on the family head to dispense traditional medicine.

What did the Romans eat? It depended on their economic level, but most Romans ate three meals daily. Ancient murals give glimpses of what was served in upper-class homes, and archaeologists have examined ancient food stores, garbage piles, and human feces for more clues. The mainstays of the lower classes were dried legumes and millet porridge. All classes enjoyed fermented fish sauces made from salted and dried fish guts.

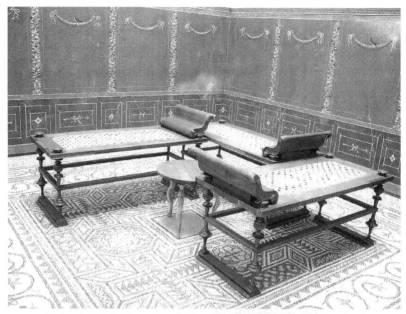

The triclinium (dining room) of elite Roman homes had couches and small tables.

Upper-class Romans ate a diet similar to today's Mediterranean diet; it featured fish, shellfish, cheese, eggs, chickens, pheasants, and other birds for protein. They ate legumes, bread, and a wide array of vegetables and fruits, such as apples, beans, grapes, onions, pears, and olives. They cherished cabbage as a source of good health. They had no tomatoes, as those originated in South America and weren't introduced until much later. With no ovens in the home for baking, they purchased bread from bakeries.

Rome was established as an agricultural community, where most men served dual roles as farmers and soldiers. By the time of the Roman Republic, these were still the two primary occupations. They also had more specialized careers, primarily employing plebeians, such as accountants, architects, artists, bankers, construction workers, craftsmen, doctors, engineers, entertainers, fishermen, government officials, jewelers, merchants, shopkeepers, sailors, teachers, tax collectors, and smiths.

Roman tradition held that senators should be farmers who occasionally served the state. Senators who commanded military legions often became the governors of new provinces they brought into the republic. The governmental changes in the republic required the senators to spend more time dealing with administrative tasks and financial and military decisions, as well as organizing diplomatic missions. The senators still owned their farms; in fact, as Rome conquered new lands, the senators and other patricians acquired huge plantations. But they usually had a land manager and dozens or hundreds of enslaved people working the fields.

At the beginning of the Roman Republic, the senators were all from the patrician class and felt that work in trade and commerce was déclassé, fit only for the plebeians. Furthermore, engaging in business could present a conflict of interest in politics. They even had laws restricting senators' engagement in commodities; for instance, they couldn't own a merchant ship.[11] But they found ways around the law, becoming silent partners and investors in business ventures, as they were unwilling to let the plebeians reap all the vast riches available in commerce. Once plebeians became part of the Senate, class lines began to blur.

A huge issue during the republic was unemployment, which was primarily due to previous tenant farmers being displaced by slave labor on the plantations. Toward the end of the republic, more than 300,000 people had gravitated toward Rome in hopes of finding work, to no avail. Sometimes, Rome sent these unemployed farmers and other unemployed workers to new colonies it established around the Mediterranean.

Freedmen (freed slaves) competed with these displaced farmers; they sometimes had more advanced skills, depending on their previous occupation or education before becoming enslaved. They also had the patronage of their former owners, which could open doors of opportunity.[12] Freedmen often worked as bakers, carpenters, and in the fish trade, while their wives worked as midwives, hairdressers, or seamstresses.

---

[11] Lionel Casson, *Everyday Life in Ancient Rome*, (Baltimore: Johns Hopkins University Press, 1998), 48-56.

[12] Cory R DiBacco, "The Position of Freedmen in Roman Society," *MAD-RUSH Undergraduate Research Conference*, (Spring 2017), JMU Scholarly Commons. https://commons.lib.jmu.edu/cgi/viewcontent.cgi?article=1069&context=madrush.

What gender roles did men and women have in the Roman Republic? Rome was clearly male-dominated. The husband and/or father was the undisputed master of the home. Husbands openly had mistresses, visited prostitutes, and had sexual relationships with adolescent boys who were usually slaves or freed slaves. Male same-sex relationships were socially acceptable as long as the older man was the dominant partner with a male of lower social status.

A woman's primary role was the caretaker of the home and raising children. She was expected to be a virgin before marriage and chaste afterward. Fathers arranged marriages for their daughters, and a woman could use either her husband's surname or her father's surname after marriage.

Upper-class girls went to school but not as long as boys did. They could read and write and were knowledgeable in literature and philosophy. Girls from poor families did not attend school, although their brothers might. Plebeian women were out in public much more than aristocratic women because many had jobs. They could be shopkeepers, hairdressers, midwives, and craftworkers.

If a woman had legal or financial affairs that needed attention, even with inherited property, she usually had to have a male relative take care of it. However, widows had more freedom to manage their business affairs. By Roman law, a woman's property could not be comingled with her husband's, and if they divorced, she got it back. Unfortunately, she did not get custody of her children if she divorced.

Slavery in Rome and its territories experienced exponential growth during the republican era, as Rome conquered massive territories and brought back enslaved prisoners of war. Enslaved people in Rome came from many races; some had been highly educated or skilled in specific crafts in their home country. Aside from prisoners of war, some enslaved people were sailors captured at sea by pirates and sold in the slave market. Slaves could also be Roman; sometimes, impoverished parents sold their children to pay debts or because they could not feed them.

Slave labor included field workers, household servants, skilled craftsmen, architects, engineers, teachers, and scribes; it all depended on their skills and education. Rome had no laws protecting enslaved people from abuse or even murder by their masters. However, some slave owners allowed their slaves to buy their freedom or even set them free with no strings attached and assisted them in adapting to life as freedmen.

Some slaves became gladiators, like those depicted in the Zliten mosaic.
https://commons.wikimedia.org/wiki/File:Gladiators_from_the_Zliten_mosaic_3.JPG

Spartacus, a captured soldier from Thrace, became a gladiator, which often happened to prisoners of war with military experience. Romans flocked to the Forum (the Colosseum wasn't built until the early imperial era) to watch the gory matches. While being a gladiator had its glamorous moments, the combatants weren't enthusiastic about their short lifespan. So, one night in 73 BCE, Spartacus and seventy-eight fellow gladiators grabbed their chance to escape, arming themselves with knives from the kitchen.

They made their way to Mount Vesuvius, which had been dormant for centuries but would explode 152 years later and bury Pompeii. Other enslaved people joined them on their journey, and the escapees plundered fields and villages, accumulating weapons and food. The Roman praetor Claudius Glaber marched to Vesuvius with a force of three thousand, intending to trap the runaways at the top of the mountain and starve them out.

But the intrepid slaves made rope ladders from vines and escaped down the cliff to the valley below. They traipsed through Italy, freeing enslaved people from plantations, storming Roman units by surprise, and building their weapons supply as their numbers escalated to seventy thousand. The vagabonds split up when two consuls leading separate legions pursued them. Part of them stayed in southern Italy and fell to the Roman army, but the rest hiked into northern Italy with Spartacus. The plan was to cross the Alps out of Italy, and then everyone could return to their home countries. (There are many different theories as to why Spartacus chose to go south and why the slaves split into two groups, but these are the most popular theories.)

When they got to the Alps, most runaways lost heart at the sight of the ten-thousand-foot peaks. It was spring, and the snow cap hadn't melted enough to cross over. They worried that if they stayed, they might get trapped against the mountains. They decided to march south, cross the straits to Sicily, and stir up the enslaved people there, who had revolted a couple of decades earlier. They were confident they could take Sicily and hold it against the Romans. They reached the straits and paid pirates to take them across, but the pirates sailed off with their money, leaving them behind.

The Roman commander Crassus thought he had Spartacus trapped in the toe of Italy's boot. He built a thirty-seven-mile canal across the peninsula and a wall behind the channel to keep the slaves from escaping. But Spartacus's followers dammed the canal, crossed over, and scaled the wall. At this point, the escapees were at odds regarding their next step. They split up, leaving Spartacus with a much smaller group. Their overconfidence after winning one battle against the Roman legion spelled their death, as they succumbed to the Romans in the next fight. The Romans crucified the six thousand who survived the battle; their gory crosses spread one hundred miles along the Appian Way from Capua to Rome.

Chapter 4: Literature, Art, and Religion

In the heel of Italy's boot lay Tarentum, a Greek city, one of the largest in the world in its day. It had the most powerful naval fleet and ground forces in southern Italy, and with its lucrative trade, it was unimaginably wealthy. But in 209 BCE, it fell to Rome. The Romans slaughtered thousands and pillaged the city's priceless artwork, carrying the treasures off to Rome along with thirty thousand enslaved people.

Among those thirty thousand was Andronicus, a scholarly and cultured young man. Realizing his value, a Roman general named Marcus Livius Salinator purchased him to tutor his children. Taking his master's family name, Livius Andronicus translated Greek masterpieces like Homer's *Odyssey* into Latin to instruct Salinator's children. Salinator later set Andronicus free, and Andronicus established his own school and wrote tragedies and comedies for the stage. He became the first known writer of epic poetry and dramatic works in the Latin language.

This Pompeii mosaic depicts Livius Andronicus, Rome's first Latin writer.
https://commons.wikimedia.org/wiki/File:Pompeii_-_Casa_del_Poeta_Tragico_-_Theater_3.jpg

The Roman Republic's early writers were often educated Greek slaves, freedmen like Andronicus, or the Roman students they taught. Many educated Romans spoke Greek and studied Greek philosophy and satire. The Golden Age of Latin literature during the republic's last seventy years was a time of intense cultural advancement in Rome, despite civil wars and political collapse. Distinctive Roman styles marked Rome's remarkable literary accomplishments during the Golden Age.

Rome's Golden Age writers included Cicero, a political philosopher desperate to solve Rome's multiple crises. He wrote many treatises that supported the old patrician aristocracy, tried to repair the constitution, and defended peace and order. He asserted that preserving life and property united the people, enabling them to achieve their maximum potential. Cooperation was the key to achieving goals and fulfilling duties, which he said was the highest good.

Publius Vergilius Maro, better known as Virgil, grew up in a farming community in northern Italy. His first collection of poems, *Eclogues* (or *Bucolics*), explored the agony of his pastoral neighbors who lost their ancestral lands in Rome's shifting political scene. Three centuries later, Emperor Constantine interpreted some lines in his fourth *Eclogues* as a prophecy of Jesus Christ: "The Virgin returns bringing the beloved King." Saint Augustine agreed with Constantine but said Virgil didn't understand his own prophecy.[13]

Virgil's epic poetry covered current issues and Roman myths.
https://commons.wikimedia.org/wiki/File:Parco_della_Grotta_di_Posillipo.5_(crop).jpg

Virgil's final and most famous work was the *Aeneid*, which is about the travels of Rome's mythical ancestor Aeneas as he escapes from the flames of Troy to finally settle in central Italy. Virgil never

---

[13] Ella Bourne, "The Messianic Prophecy in Vergil's Fourth Eclogue," *The Classical Journal* Vol. 11, No. 7, (April 1916), 390-400.
https://www.jstor.org/stable/pdf/3287925.pdf.

finished the *Aeneid*; he died while still editing it. Nevertheless, it served to rally hope in Rome's chaotic times. It has endured through the millennia as a pillar of classical education and influenced later literary works like *Beowulf*, *Paradise Lost*, and the *Divine Comedy*. The story is retold in Enthralling History's *Ancient Rome*.[14]

Publius Ovidius Naso, better known as Ovid, opted for a poet's life rather than following his patrician father into public service. His humorous poems advising on love amused the Roman population, who raved about his three-book series, *The Art of Love*. In the first book, he told men how to find a woman: "She won't fall out of thin air; you have to look for her." He suggested specific places to find a girl, like the races or the circus, where the crowded seating meant you could "press your thigh to hers." He instructed the men to pay gentlemanly attention to the young lady while perhaps catching "a glimpse of her legs." He told young men to get a decent haircut, wear a clean toga, and ensure they had no dirt under their nails, no hair sprouting from their nostrils, and no bad breath! In the second book, he told men how to keep a woman once they got one, and the third book advised women on how to find and keep a man.[15]

Ovid's most prominent work was *Metamorphosis*, a collection of fifteen books dealing with mythology and the transformations the protagonists experienced. He discusses the world's creation and the Golden Age when humans had no laws or punishments and were pure and good. Then came the Silver Age, when Saturn was banished from heaven. Humans had to work hard to plow the land and sheltered in crude houses from the cold. Because of the humans' violence, Jupiter decided to destroy all people with a great flood, but he chose one family to survive. Ovid also describes other Roman myths and the relationship between the gods and humanity in *Metamorphosis*.[16]

---

[14] Enthralling History, *Ancient Rome: An Enthralling Overview of Roman History, Starting from the Romulus and Remus Myth through the Republic to the Fall of the Roman Empire* (2021), 10-24.

[15] Ovid. *The Art of Love (Ars Amatoria)*, trans. A. S. Kline. Poetry in Translation. https://www.poetryintranslation.com/PITBR/Latin/ArtofLoveBkII.php.

[16] Ovid, *Metamorphoses*, trans. Sir Samuel Garth, John Dryden, et al. http://classics.mit.edu/Ovid/metam.1.first.html.

Art in the Roman Republic encompassed various disciplines, including marble sculptures, buildings, murals, mosaics, and silver and bronze metalworking. The republic's early artwork was not much different than during the monarchy, nor was it prolific; the Romans were utilitarian, so they were more concerned with function than aesthetics. But Rome's clashes with Greece led to a new appreciation of art.

When Rome conquered Greek cities like Corinth, the soldiers plundered priceless sculptures and other artwork to carry back to Rome. Tragically, they often damaged the pieces in transit, but the Romans copied the Greek statues and other artwork, absorbing their innovative techniques. Rome's adaptation of the Greek culture led to the Greco-Roman style, which has graced architecture and art to the present age. In the republic's last century, artists and architects began producing uniquely Roman creations, such as realistic portraits and stunning buildings.

Roman buildings were initially constructed from wood, stone, or mudbrick, but by the 2nd century BCE, Roman concrete enabled gigantic columns and free-flowing building styles to be created. Roman concrete incorporated volcanic ash, making it durable and free of cracks. Architecture generally followed Greek design, but the Romans borrowed Etruscan technology to build aqueducts. The Etruscan aqueducts were mainly in-ground uncovered channels (like a paved ditch) that drained the swampy areas or moved water from rivers for irrigation.

This Roman aqueduct in Spain used three levels of arches to span the ravine, keeping the water pipe through the top section level.

The Romans also borrowed the arch from the Etruscans. Middle Eastern countries had used the arch for centuries, but the Romans refined the above-ground arch, incorporating it into breathtaking buildings, bridges, and above-ground aqueducts. They literally took the arch to new heights! And they took the multi-arched aqueduct everywhere, as far as Spain, France, and Germany.[17] In the late republic, the Romans built the earliest monumental dome and the world's largest dome up to that point. Located close to Naples, the "Temple of Mercury" (not actually a temple) was seventy-one feet in diameter. It covered one of the public baths in the resort town of Baia and is the oldest surviving concrete dome.

---

[17] Bono, P. and C. Boni, "Water Supply of Rome in Antiquity and Today," *Geo* 27, (1996), 126–134. https://doi.org/10.1007/BF01061685.

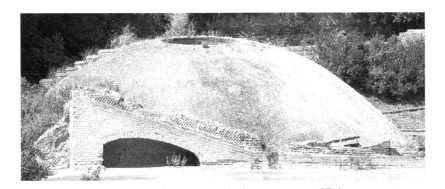
The Temple of Mercury was in the resort town of Baiae.

In the Roman Republic, only elected magistrates could commission new public buildings. Because they only had one-year terms, they could build smaller projects like temples, but grand projects were not feasible. It wasn't until the last century of the Roman Republic that politicians commissioned self-aggrandizing and extravagant architectural projects like the Forum of Caesar and the Portico of Pompey.[18]

The Temple of Portunus, built in the 1st century BCE, exemplifies Roman Republican architecture. It was constructed of limestone and porous volcanic tuff with a plaster covering meant to resemble Greek marble. The frieze decorations on the upper pillars and roof feature garlands and an ox-skull motif. The temple dedicated to the water god Portunus was converted into a church in the 9th century CE, preserving it from the destruction of temples and fine buildings that occurred during the Dark Ages.

---

[18] Penelope E. Davies, *Architecture and Politics in Republican Rome* (Cambridge: Cambridge University Press, 2017), 2-4.

Elegant carvings graced the "capital" (top) of the pillars in the Temple to Portunus.

Benjamín Núñez González, CC BY-SA 4.0 <https://creativecommons.org/licenses/by-sa/4.0>, via Wikimedia Commons; https://commons.wikimedia.org/wiki/File:Detalles_del_Templo_de_Portuno,_Roma,_2017_04.jpg

Romans carved exquisite columns and sculptures from translucent white marble. They enjoyed adding color to their designs with colored marble and other semi-precious materials. Artists decorated the faces of sculptures with paint and gilding and sometimes painted the entire statue. Color was as essential to Roman sculpture as the fluid form.[19]

Sculptures of this era had a marked Hellenistic (Greek) influence and were usually lifelike portrayals of Roman leaders carved in marble and bronze. These sculptures featured incredible realism. They included people's imperfections, such as warts, wrinkles, sagging jowls, scowls, and huge, hooked noses. It seemed to reflect the Romans' intent to sensibly observe reality and the understanding that the leaders democratically representing the people *were* people, with all their frailties.

---

[19] Mark B. Abbe, "Polychromy of Roman Marble Sculpture," in *Heilbrunn Timeline of Art History* (New York: The Metropolitan Museum of Art, 2007) http://www.metmuseum.org/toah/hd/prms/hd_prms.htm.

This marble bust reveals Cato the Elder in stark realism.
https://commons.wikimedia.org/wiki/File:Patrizio_Torlonia.jpg

When Mount Vesuvius erupted in 79 CE, it killed thousands of people and buried Pompeii and nearby cities under twenty feet of volcanic ash and pumice. This covering preserved the city for two millennia, so recent excavations have revealed breathtaking paintings and mosaics from the late republic and early imperial ages. Many Greek painters relocated to Italy in the late republic; they were hired by aristocratic families to decorate their dining rooms and atriums with wall frescoes. Some of these paintings were copies of original Greek works from a century or more prior. Mosaic tile art emerged in Rome and its colonies in the 3rd century BCE. First used as a practical yet decorative floor covering, mosaics later covered walls with intricate and realistic scenes.

This 2nd-century BCE Pompeii mosaic warned, "Cave Canem" ("Beware the dog").

Virgil's *Aeneid* records that Rome's ancestors worshiped two household gods called the Penates. They were lifelike male images and small enough for Aeneas's father to cling to while he was carried on Aeneas's back in the escape from Troy. The Penates guided Aeneas in his wanderings, redirecting him to Italy when he made a wrong turn to Crete. Dionysius reported that after settling in Lavinium (nineteen miles south of what would be Rome), Aeneas constructed a shrine for the Penates at the top of the city's hill. They were no longer household gods but deities and guardians for all the refugees, an embodiment of their Trojan past.

This republican era denarius struck in 106 BCE shows the two Penates (left); on the other side is a scene from the Aeneid where Aeneas finds the prophesied white sow.

Johny SYSEL, CC BY-SA 3.0 <https://creativecommons.org/licenses/by-sa/3.0>, via Wikimedia Commons;

https://commons.wikimedia.org/wiki/File:AR_serrate_denarius_of_C._Sulpicius_C._f._Galba.jpg

Curiously, Virgil said that after Aeneas's son Ascanius built Alba Longa and moved most of his population there, he made a shrine for the Penates at Alba Longa, but they didn't want to stay there. He woke up in the morning to find them gone, and someone reported they had returned to Lavinium. How the Penates got there was a mystery. Finally, Ascanius gave up and let them stay in Lavinium in his father's shrine. Lavinium persisted as a sacred city through the Roman Republic; newly elected consuls and praetors traveled there from Rome to bring sacrifices to the Penates.

From Rome's inception, it was polytheistic, adopting gods from Greece and other countries. Aeneas brought the worship of Vesta, the virgin goddess of the family and hearth, from Troy, and her worship continued throughout the republic. The sacred temple fire tended by the Vestal Virgins represented her rather than images. Unlike the typical Roman and Greek deities, Vesta had few myths and did not engage in feuds with other gods. Other chief gods were Jupiter (the Greek Zeus), king of the gods; his wife Juno (the Greek Hera), goddess of the moon and fertility; the sea-god Neptune (the Greek Poseidon); and Mars (the Greek Ares), the god of war.

The Romans practiced animal sacrifice. They preferred to sacrifice pigs but also offered sheep and oxen. Human sacrifice was rare, but in the struggle against Hannibal in 216 BCE, Livy recorded the sacrifice of human victims, probably enslaved people, from France and Greece:

"By the direction of the Books of Fate, some unusual sacrifices were offered; amongst others a Gaulish man and woman and a Greek man and woman were buried alive in the Cattle Market, in a place walled in with stone, which even before this time had been defiled with human victims, a sacrifice wholly alien to the Roman spirit."[20]

During the monarchy, the king held priestly duties, but during the Roman Republic, a patrician took on those religious responsibilities in a lifelong position called *rex sacrorum* ("king of the priests"). Rome also had an elected chief priest over the state clergy (the College of Pontiffs) called *pontifex maximus*, the pope's title today. Different religions had their own *flamines* (high priests of a cult). The rest of the priests were part-time positions held by men and women of high social standing.

During the republican era, the Romans did not interfere with the religions of conquered countries; they sometimes even assimilated them. What they believed was not as crucial as their active involvement in religious rites. The Romans believed their divine right to rule over much of the known world came from their dedication to religion and the understanding that the gods control everything.

---

[20] Livius, *History of Rome, Vol. V.*

PART TWO: Warfare and Expansion (350–200 BCE)

Chapter 5: The Roman Army

How did the Romans manage to conquer lands stretching from the Middle East to North Africa and into western Europe? How did they accomplish incredible success without initially being tactically and technologically unremarkable? Part of their phenomenal triumph flowed from their indomitable, dogged nature. They refused to accept defeat, even in the face of military catastrophes. Sheer unwavering determination enabled the Romans to achieve victories, despite the odds stacked against them.

Throughout the centuries of the Roman Republic, the Roman military retained its tenacity but matured and evolved into an insurmountable military machine. To what do we credit Rome's inconceivable achievements on land and at sea? Military organization, rigid discipline, rewards for bravery, siege warfare technology, ingenious tactics, and formidable weaponry all played a decisive part.

How were soldiers recruited into the army? Who could serve, and for how long? In the early republic, soldiers were conscripts, mostly from Rome, although an additional one thousand soldiers were provided from the Etruscan, Latin, and Sabine tribes. To serve in the army, a Roman citizen had to be a landowner. Most soldiers were also farmers, so their deployments were only for a brief period, usually between spring planting and fall harvest—the traditional war season. Although they might spend time training in the winter or when no wars were going on, they were generally only called up for specific conflicts. The troops disbanded whenever a military campaign ended; the early republic had no standing army.

When General Marius ran for consul in 107 BCE, his campaign promise was a swift and victorious end to the war dragging out with Numidia in North Africa. When he won, he realized Rome didn't have enough soldiers because there weren't enough property owners. Marius received the Senate's permission to recruit plebeian men who didn't own property. Rather than drafting military personnel, he felt that volunteer soldiers were more willing to fight. He especially preferred to recruit veterans with fighting experience.[21]

Marius's military reforms also included the government paying for soldiers' basic armor and weapons. This was the beginning of Rome's standing army. Two decades later, Rome was still short of soldiers, so it recruited from other tribes in Italy, rewarding them with citizenship at the end of their service. With Romans and non-Romans serving together for months, a new culture emerged in the military, one that was loyal to Rome rather than their home cities and tribes.

One hundred Roman soldiers (later eighty) formed a group called a century. Six centuries formed a cohort. Ten cohorts made up a legion, which would consist of 4,800 to 6,000 men depending on the size of the century. Livius said that in 362 BCE, Rome had two legions, each led by one of the consuls. By 311 BCE, the number grew to four legions, enabling Rome to defeat the Samnites after decades of war. More legions empowered Rome to fight on multiple fronts in the ensuing Pyrrhic and Punic Wars.

As Rome began to fight outside of Italy, in lands thousands of miles away, it needed soldiers who could commit to long-term deployments. Thus, the part-time, mostly volunteer army morphed into a standing army with legions positioned around the Mediterranean. By the end of the Roman Republic, Rome had more than twenty legions stationed at permanent bases. Each legion usually had a 120-horse cavalry, which was used more for scouting and carrying messages than fighting.

---

[21] Andrew Lintott, "Political History, 146–95 BC," in *The Cambridge Ancient History*, ed. by John Crook, Andrew Lintott, and Elizabeth Rawson (Cambridge: Cambridge University Press, 1992), 92.

The Jewish historian and military commander Josephus described the Roman army as highly skillful in war, well organized, and fighting with elegant unity. Impeccably armed, they unhesitatingly followed their leaders' clear-headed orders. Josephus said their rigid discipline enabled even a smaller force to prevail over larger, more disorganized units. Lastly, the Romans were tireless in battle, stoically pressing on until they achieved their objective.[22]

The Romans used a variety of siege engines to break down city gates, thick high walls, and other fortifications. Some siege towers and catapults were on wheels and could be rolled up to the city walls. Siege ladders enabled soldiers to scale the walls. Engineers built trenches and defensive walls to protect the soldiers from arrows launched from the city and dug tunnels under the walls.

As commander of the Jewish forces when Rome besieged Lower Galilee, Josephus gave a firsthand account of the devastation wrought by the Roman siege engines. Most of the Jewish army had holed up in the city of Jotapata (Yodfat), which sat on the top of a precipice encircled by a heavy wall. The Romans began their assault by cutting down hundreds of trees and gathering stones and earth to build a bank against the city wall. They worked in the "tortoise formation," with a shield wall protecting them from arrows shot from atop the city walls.

Rome ballista of 1 talent caliber

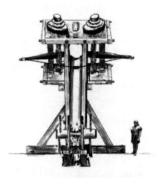

The ballista's levers with torsion springs launched stones five hundred yards.
https://commons.wikimedia.org/wiki/File:Bal_BBC1.jpg

---

[22] Flavius Josephus, *The Jewish War*, Book III, Chapter 1. http://penelope.uchicago.edu/josephus/war-3.html.

The bank enabled the Romans to get their 160 catapults high enough to fire huge rocks into the city, along with arrows shot by their allied Arabian forces. Vespasian then brought his battering ram into play, a massive wooden beam with an iron ram's head at the end, slung through the air by ropes. Many men pulled the ram backward, then flung it forward, smashing the wall with the iron head.

The Galileans screamed as the walls around them shook. But the Jews fended off the battering ram by dropping bags of chaff on ropes on the part of the wall being attacked by the ram, softening the blows. Other Jews snuck out by night and set fire to the siege engines. Yet the Romans maintained order, rebuilt their equipment, and continued the siege. The battering ram and rocks thrown by the catapults began crumbling the walls and striking the people inside.

The Galileans blunted the battering ram's swing propulsion with bags of chaff.
Rijksmuseum, CC0, via Wikimedia Commons:
https://commons.wikimedia.org/wiki/File:Beleg_van_Jotapata_door_de_Romeinen_onder_Vespasianus_RP-P-1896-A-19368-2321.jpg

One massive rock hit a pregnant woman in the belly, expelling the fetus from her body. Another boulder hit a man standing next to Josephus, decapitating him and flinging his head far away. The streets were slippery with blood as the dead bodies piled up. The Romans rushed the wall's breaches with a resounding trumpet blast and a loud shout. But the Jews poured scalding oil on them, and the Romans fell away, screaming as the hot oil seeped into their helmets and armor.

Yet, the indefatigable Romans behind them pressed in, calling anyone who faltered a coward. Vespasian had his men erect three fifty-foot towers covered with iron plates and filled them with archers. He rolled these up the embankment against the wall, along with the catapults. The Galileans abandoned the city walls as the Roman arrows darkened the sky. The city finally fell. Forty thousand Jews died in battle or by suicide, and the Romans enslaved twelve hundred women and children.[23]

What were the expectations for a Roman soldier? They needed immense physical strength and the ability to endure hardship, such as long marches while carrying all their gear. They had to obey any commands their superiors gave them instantly. Insubordinate or cowardly soldiers were mercilessly punished, often by death. The generals recognized the soldiers who displayed unusual courage on the battlefield or performed exemplary feats. Polybius said the general would give a speech lauding the soldiers who stood out in battle and then hand out rewards. Anyone who wounded the enemy got a spear. The first soldier to scale the wall of a city under siege got a gold crown.

"For the recipients of such gifts, quite apart from becoming famous in the army and famous too for the time at their homes, are especially distinguished in religious processions after their return, as no one is allowed to wear decorations except those on whom the consul has conferred these honors for bravery; and in their houses they hang up the spoils they won in the most conspicuous places, looking upon them as tokens and evidence of their courage. Considering all this attention given to the matter of punishments and rewards in the army and the importance attached to both, no wonder that the wars in which the Romans engage end so successfully and brilliantly."[24]

---

[23] Josephus, *The Jewish War*, Book III, Chapter 7.
[24] Polybius, *The Histories*, Vol. 6, Sect. 6.
http://penelope.uchicago.edu/Thayer/E/Roman/Texts/Polybius/home.html.

The standard weapons for a Roman soldier were a spear, a sword, and a dagger. The *pilum* was a six-and-a-half-foot spear weighing between two to five pounds with a wooden shaft and an iron shank. The *pilum* was hurled at the enemy rather than being used in hand-to-hand combat and was famous for piercing through armor. After fighting on the Iberian Peninsula in the Punic Wars, the Romans adopted the iron *gladius Hispaniensis*, or Spanish sword, in the 2nd century BCE. This sword was ideal for hand-to-hand combat on a packed battlefield, as its twenty-five-inch blade was shorter and easier to use for stabbing and slashing.

The *pugio* dagger was a sidearm commonly carried both on the battlefield and by officials going about their tasks in Rome. It was a handy defensive tool in battle if the soldier lost his sword and spear. In civilian life, it was a weapon of assassination and suicide. Officials often concealed it in their toga in case they needed to kill a rival or defend themselves from attack.

During the Roman Republic, soldiers carried a round *scutum* shield, which was later replaced by a large rectangular shield in the imperial age. The middle of the shield had a boss, a rounded or conical-shaped protrusion of bronze or iron. This type of shield would effectively deflect blows when the soldier used a punching motion; he could also use it as an offensive weapon to smash an opponent.

A soldier usually had chainmail armor in the republican era; the armor was formed by tiny rings of iron linked together to form a flexible and breathable cover. Some soldiers wore scale armor with iron or bronze scales sewn into the cloth so the scales overlapped. The typical helmet for most soldiers at this time was the Montefortino, adopted from the Celts, which resembled a metal baseball cap worn backward.

The Montefortino helmet was popular in the Roman Republic.

Roman commanders had multiple tactics in their repertoire. In the earlier republic, the soldiers lined up in a formation similar to a Greek phalanx. Rows of soldiers stood shoulder to shoulder, with their shields slightly overlapping, forming a shield wall. This formation protected the front line from enemy projectiles. The multiple rows of soldiers pushed those in front of them with their shields, turning the whole mass into a human bulldozer that could trample an opposing army.

The Romans later implemented their twist of the Macedonian phalanx, which was developed by Philip II, the father of Alexander the Great. By 315 BCE, the Romans used a manipular formation composed of multiple groups or maniples of 120 men. Rather than a solid line, each smaller unit operated independently. The front lines had fifteen maniples or groups, followed by another fifteen maniples, and then finally fifteen *principes*, groups of older military veterans. Each section had a junior commander who could direct the troops according to the moment's need rather than waiting for the general's order.

Plutarch told the story of one battle in the Pyrrhic Wars where the Romans faced a Macedonian phalanx that seemed impenetrable. But the Roman junior commander grabbed his company's standard and threw it into the middle of the adversary's phalanx. The standard had a bronze eagle or some other similar figure atop a long pole. The soldiers rallied around their standard and protected it at all costs. When they saw it flung among the enemy, they immediately surged forward to rescue it, breaking the enemy's phalanx. Both sides suffered horrendous casualties.

Romans began using carrier pigeons in the Roman Republic to send messages. Spies in Mark Antony's camp sent messages to Brutus via pigeon that helped him devise a successful strategy based on his inside information about the enemy. The Romans also sometimes set booby traps for their adversaries. In one battle, a commander named Quintus Sertorius faced a cavalry much larger than his. That night, he dug trenches all over, then faced off against the enemy. His men moved their horses to the side when they charged, letting the enemy surge through right into the ditches!

In the First Punic War, the Romans realized that prevailing over Carthage in North Africa required a navy. The Greeks, Egyptians, and ancient Phoenicians of Carthage and Lebanon had ruled the waves for over a millennium. Rome had merchant ships but no navy and no master shipbuilders. But that didn't stop the irrepressible Romans. They inspected a Carthaginian quinquereme that had washed ashore in a storm. Using it as a model, they built one hundred warships in only two months!

Rome celebrated military victories with a triumph, a dazzling parade and ceremony that lasted an entire day. It began with the conquering commander, dressed in purple and wearing a laurel crown, giving speeches and distributing rewards and money to his men. Then, a grand procession would proceed through the city accompanied by flag-wavers and musicians. The people cheered at the sight of the commander in his chariot, as well as the plundered treasures and royal captives led in gold chains.

The Romans seemed unrefined by the standards of the Greeks and other ancient civilizations. Yet, the unsophisticated "barbarians" possessed a dynamic spirit that developed a well-oiled military machine that soon ruled the Mediterranean. Rome's conquests during the Roman Republic brought tremendous political power and astounding wealth to Italy. By the end of the republic, it had spawned the Pax Romana: domestic peace around the Mediterranean that permitted a flourishing trade and an enriching exchange of cultures.

Chapter 6: Greek and Roman Relations

For over a century, Rome squared off with the remnants of Alexander the Great's empire in a fierce quest for dominance over the Mediterranean. First, Pyrrhus of Epirus came to "assist" southern Italy's Greek cities as they wrestled with Rome. Next, Rome inserted itself into the Greek world's convoluted politics while simultaneously struggling with Hannibal and other Carthaginians in the Punic Wars.

King Pyrrhus became famous for his costly "pyrrhic victories" against Rome. After his second technical win, he groaned, "If we are victorious in one more battle with the Romans, we shall be utterly ruined."[25]

The Pyrrhic Wars entangled Rome with the Greek city-states of southern Italy, their allied Italian tribes, and the Macedonian-Greek world to the east. In 282 BCE, Roman ships sailed into the Gulf of Taranto in southernmost Italy, which was off-limits to Rome based on a treaty with the massive city of Tarentum. Why were the Romans in the forbidden bay? They were transporting troops to a Roman garrison in Thurii, a Greek city allied with Rome.

---

[25] Plutarch, *The Parallel Lives*, Volume IX, "The Life of Pyrrhus."

The indignant Tarentines considered this intrusion an act of war, so they attacked and sunk four transport ships and captured one. They then sailed to Thurii and incited a democratic revolution, influencing the population to eject the Roman garrison. Rome responded by declaring war on Tarentum, so the Tarentines called on King Pyrrhus of Epirus (Albania) across the Adriatic Sea.

King Pyrrhus of Epirus had empire-building ambitions.
Classical Numismatic Group, Inc. http://www.cngcoins.com, CC BY-SA 2.5 <https://creativecommons.org/licenses/by-sa/2.5>, via Wikimedia Commons; https://commons.wikimedia.org/wiki/File:Pyrrhus_Kingdom_of_Epirus.JPG

King Pyrrhus had delusions of grandeur; he imagined reigning over an empire like his cousin Alexander the Great. He came to Tarentum's aid, thinking he could gain a foothold in Italy, despite his insufficient resources for a military campaign. He borrowed ships from King Antigonus of Macedonia and funding from Antiochus of the Seleucid Empire. Pharoah Ptolemy of Egypt loaned him soldiers, horses, and twenty war elephants.[26]

Overly eager, Pyrrhus crossed the Adriatic before spring, but a fierce winter storm decimated part of his forces. Then, Pyrrhus realized the Tarentines wanted him to fight their battles while they enjoyed drinking bouts and festivities. Pyrrhus outlawed revelry and drunkenness and drafted the men for military service. Some left town, unwilling to fight and disgruntled at losing their freedom.

---

[26] N. G. L. Hammond, "Which Ptolemy Gave Troops and Stood as Protector of Pyrrhus' Kingdom?" *Historia: Zeitschrift Für Alte Geschichte* 37, no. 4 (1988): 405. http://www.jstor.org/stable/4436071.

The Romans mobilized thirty thousand men and marched south to attack Pyrrhus. Pyrrhus met them at the Siris River with thirty-five thousand troops, three thousand cavalry, and twenty elephants. He viewed the Roman camp from a high bluff and admired their discipline and order. At first light, the Romans charged across the river, and Pyrrhus met the most ferocious army he'd ever encountered.

In a panic, he exchanged his armor with his lieutenant, fearing the Romans would target him. He was right: they killed the hapless lieutenant wearing the king's battle gear. Pyrrhus swung the battle by sending his elephants charging toward the Romans, who had never seen such enormous animals. Their frenzied horses raced off the field, and Pyrrhus's cavalry quickly scattered the petrified Roman soldiers.

Pyrrhus won the battle but not before a wounded elephant stampeded his own troops, leaving mangled bodies in its wake. Up to fifteen thousand Romans and thirteen thousand Macedonian and Greeks perished that day. However, Rome still had tens of thousands of troops in southern Italy. Pyrrhus was relieved when some of the Italian tribes and Italy's Greek city-states replenished his forces.

While both sides regrouped, Pyrrhus's physician Nicias sent a letter to the Romans, offering to poison Pyrrhus in exchange for a reward. The outraged Consul Fabricius sputtered that Rome would win through tenacity, tactics, and toughness, not poison! He alerted Pyrrhus of Nicias's plot, who thanked Fabricius by releasing his Roman prisoners of war. Pyrrhus killed and flayed Nicias, using his skin to form the straps of a chair.

Pyrrhus met Rome's army with forty thousand men in the gruesome Battle of Asculum, which raged for two days. The rough, forested terrain hindered elephant and cavalry charges. Rome had created three hundred anti-elephant wagons pulled by oxen. Spears projected out from iron beams, and the wagons carried catapults that launched fire missiles and rocks at the Greeks and their elephants.

Pyrrhus's elephants circumnavigated the wagons on the second day and chased Rome's panicked horses off the field. The battle ended with at least 6,000 dead Romans and 3,500 Greek casualties.

However, Pyrrhus had a spear wound, and the Romans looted his camp and killed most of his commanders. It was indeed a pyrrhic victory, as it was hardly worth the hollow win.

Part of Pyrrhus's long-term empire-building plan was to conquer Sicily, using it to launch a campaign against Carthage in North Africa. He leaped at an offer from Sicily's Greek city of Syracuse: "Protect us from Carthage, rid us of tyrants, and you can be our king."

The Tarentines seethed when Pyrrhus abandoned the Roman war. "Finish what you started here, or put our city back the way you found it and leave permanently!"

The Romans chuckled; now, they could subdue the Samnites, Bruttians, and Lucanians (all of which were ancient Italic tribes) who had fought on Pyrrhus's side. Rome used this interlude to conquer all the Greek city-states in southern Italy except for Tarentum and Regi. Meanwhile, Pyrrhus's plot to rule Sicily was a dismal failure. The Carthaginians outnumbered and outpowered him and drove him off the island.

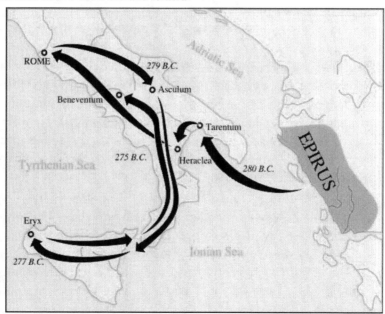

This map shows Pyrrhus's route from Epirus to Italy to Sicily and back.

Pyrrhus returned to Italy in 276 BCE with only twenty thousand men. Despite having lost his Italian and Greek allies' support, he confidently marched toward the Roman encampment at Maleventum. Maleventum meant "bad omen" or "unfortunate arrival," which struck true for Pyrrhus's bungled arrival and the ensuing debacle. Planning a surprise attack, Pyrrhus marched his men at night through the woods, but they wandered off the trail in the dark.

At sunrise, they emerged from the woods on a high bluff in full view of the Roman camp, losing the element of surprise. They were exhausted and dehydrated, and the elephants were irritable. Before they could rest and regroup, the Romans charged up the hill. Many of Pyrrhus's men chose that moment to flee. Pyrrhus's war elephants forced the Romans back, but the Romans had learned to spear the elephants in the side. The panicked and pain-crazed elephants reversed course, charging straight toward Pyrrhus and trampling the troops.

Pyrrhus couldn't even score a pyrrhic victory this time. He escaped to Tarentum, then sailed home, leaving behind the chair made from Nicias's skin. He died three years later when an old woman threw a tile at him from a rooftop. When the news reached Italy, Tarentum and Regi surrendered to Rome, giving the Romans complete control of all of Italy except for the far northern border, which was held by the Gauls.

Six decades later, Rome fought in Greece for the first time. Alexander the Great's empire had split into the Egyptian, Macedonian, and Seleucid Empires. As Egypt faltered, the Macedonians and Seleucids made a power grab. King Philip V of Macedonia didn't like Rome's involvement with Epirus and Illyria (today's Albania, Montenegro, Bosnia, and Croatia); he planned to incorporate them into Macedonia.

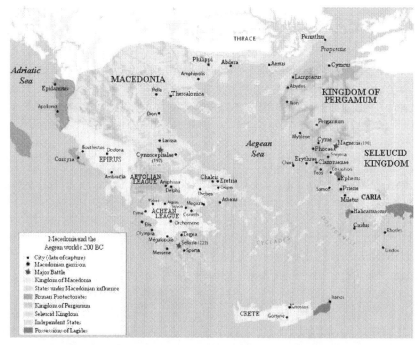

This map shows the regions involved in the Macedonian Wars.

The conflict between Philip V and Rome led to the First Macedonian War (214-205 BCE) when Philip attacked Apollonia, located in Illyria. The Romans chased him off, but Philip was back a year later, capturing two important fortresses. Rome allied with central Greece's Aetolian League and King Attalus of Pergamum (today's western Turkey). The joint forces captured the cities of Nasus, Oeniadae, Zakynthos, and Anticyra on Greece's mainland.

Philip allied with Bithynia (northern Turkey on the Black Sea) to drive the Aetolian League out of northern Greece. Philip won this conflict, but Rome's fleet sailed in just as they were negotiating the terms of surrender. However, Philip prevailed over Rome before leaving to deal with a Dardanian invasion of Macedonia. Rome moved its ships into the Adriatic Sea, focusing on protecting its trade allies by stationing ten thousand infantry and a thousand cavalry in Illyria.

Philip returned to attack the Aetolian League, driving them out of Ionia and Thessaly. After hearing that Rome was beating Carthage in the Second Punic War, Philip decided to end his war in

Greece before Rome had more resources to use in the fight against him. The Aetolian League, Macedonia, and Rome agreed to the Peace of Phoenice in 205. Philip now held part of mainland Greece and inland Illyria, but Rome was confident that coastal Illyria was safe.

The Second Macedonian War (200–197 BCE) began with a plot to grab Egypt. Ptolemy IV had died, leaving his six-year-old son, Ptolemy V, as pharaoh, and the royal family was squabbling over who would be regent. Philip V of Macedonia and Antiochus the Great of the Seleucid Empire conspired to take advantage of the chaos and divide the Egyptian territory between themselves. Antiochus would get Egypt and Cyprus, while Philip would get Cyrene and Egypt's territories in the Aegean Sea.

First, Philip needed to secure the Greek colonies near the Dardanelles Strait, which were critical to shipping traffic between the Aegean and Black Seas. Meanwhile, Antiochus conquered Sidon, Damascus, and Samaria. Philip began his Aegean Sea campaign by defeating Miletus and attacking Egypt's naval base at Samos in 201 BCE. Antiochus drove the Egyptians out of Judea, and the jubilant Jews hailed him as their conquering hero. Their joy turned to horror three decades later when Antiochus's son, Epiphanes, installed an image of Zeus in Jerusalem's temple and sacrificed a pig, sparking the Maccabean Revolt.

Rome finally triumphed over Carthage in 201 BCE and now had time to focus on Greece and Macedonia. Rome warned Philip V to withdraw his troops from Greece, leave Egypt alone, and stop aggressive actions in other regions. Philip ignored this stipulation by attacking Abydos in the Dardanelles. When all hope was lost, the men of Abydos killed their families, threw the city's treasures into the sea, and fought to the last man. Rome did not want Philip to control the Dardanelle Strait, so it declared war.

The newly elected consul, Sulpicius, sailed east with his exhausted troops, who had just returned from a lengthy deployment against Carthage. He confronted Philip in 200 BCE, but after two inconclusive battles, Philip left in the middle of the night to defend Macedonia against a Dardanian invasion. Sulpicius chased after him initially but then decided to attack the Macedonian naval bases.

In 199 BCE, Rome elected the twenty-nine-year-old Titus Quinctius Flamininus as consul, despite the age requirement of forty-one. Flamininus replaced Sulpicius and proved to be a stellar leader. He quickly freed the territory Philip had taken in Greece. He faced off with Philip at a pass in Albania. After a shepherd revealed an alternative route through the mountains, Flamininus attacked Philip's rearguard in a surprise attack, killing two thousand Macedonians.

The Senate was so pleased with Flaminius that they told him to keep fighting, even though his term as consul was about to end. Flamininus had twenty war elephants in the 197 BCE Battle of Cynoscephalae in Thessaly, which was fought in a valley covered with deep fog. His elephants won the day, with the Romans inflicting eight thousand Macedonian casualties. Philip finally surrendered, agreeing to give up any claim to Greece and stay in Macedonia.

Rome told Antiochus he could keep his empire and Egypt but to leave Thrace (today's Bulgaria) and stay clear of the Dardanelles. But Antiochus felt he had a hereditary claim to Thrace. Greece's Aetolian League abandoned its alliance with Rome for Antiochus, making him their commander in chief. He sailed to southern Greece's Peloponnese Peninsula to attack the Aetolian League's rival and Rome's ally, the Achaean League. But Rome sent them packing with two legions. The war segued to a naval battle in the Aegean Sea, where Antiochus lost half his ships. The final land battle in Thessaly in 197 BCE cost him half his land army. Antiochus surrendered his conquered cities and paid a war debt to Rome and Pergamum but continued ruling the colossal Seleucid Empire.

The Third Macedonian War began in 171 BCE, shortly after Philip V's son Perseus ascended Macedonia's throne. Perseus promised the Greeks he could restore their ancient power and wealth. But Pergamon's king, Eumenes II, sailed to Rome to warn it of Perseus's ambitions, strategic alliances, and his massive arms stockpile. The Romans declared war, allying with Pergamon.[27]

---

[27] Titus Livius, *The History of Rome*, Vol. VII.

Perseus won the first round in Thessaly, losing only four hundred men to Rome's two thousand in 171 BCE. He then attacked the Roman camp while most of the soldiers were away stealing grain from the nearby farmlands. The Romans hurried back and trapped Perseus in a ravine, killing eight thousand Macedonians while suffering four thousand casualties of their own. In the final 168 BCE Battle of Pydna, the Romans killed twenty thousand Macedonians and captured eleven thousand.

The Romans collected so much booty that Rome gave its citizens a huge tax break. The city celebrated the astounding victory over Macedonia with Rome's most spectacular triumph. The crowds went wild at the sight of Perseus led in chains, high-spirited soldiers wearing laurel wreaths, and Macedonia's treasures. Macedonia came under Rome's control and was divided into four republics.

In 146 BCE, Rome fought against the Achaean League, their former allies who now wanted to expand, despite Rome's wishes. Rome quickly squelched the league; in the last battle in Corinth, Rome captured or killed most of the Achaean soldiers and enslaved the women and children. The Romans pillaged Corinth's priceless artwork, hauling it back to Rome and damaging many pieces in transit. Rome usurped Greece's place as a world power, but Hellenistic influences would continue to impact Roman literature, philosophy, art, and religion for centuries.

Chapter 7: Mediterranean Conquest: The Punic Wars

"If you leave, I'll kill myself!"

Distraught, Queen Dido watched Aeneas prepare his ships for departure. After Aeneas, the ancestor of the Romans, had fled burning Troy, the gods directed him to Italy to build a new city. But as he was sailing toward Italy's mainland, a fierce storm forced his fleet southwest, driving the ships ashore in North Africa. Aeneas walked down the beach the following morning and encountered men building a city.

Aeneas learned they were Phoenicians from Tyre, led by their queen, Dido, and that the new city's name was Carthage. When Aeneas met Queen Dido, they were mutually attracted to each other and became lovers. Aeneas forgot his foreordained destiny until Jupiter sent Mercury to remind him: "Why are you wasting time in Libya? This is not why the gods rescued you from the Greeks! You are destined to rule Italy and give birth to an empire!"

Aeneas knew he couldn't disobey the gods, but Dido raged when she saw Aeneas resolutely preparing to leave. She told him, "There will be no love or treaties between your people and mine. Your descendants will have unending strife with Carthage! After I'm dead, I'll follow you with dark fires. You'll be punished, and I'll hear of it from the depths of Hades."

As Aeneas's ships sailed away during the night, Queen Dido sank into madness, unsheathing Aeneas's sword he'd left behind and plunging it into her chest.[28]

Queen Dido of Carthage cursed Aeneas before her suicide.
https://commons.wikimedia.org/wiki/File:Stallaert-Dido.jpg

Almost a millennium later, Dido's prophecy came to pass, as Rome and Carthage fought three legendary wars against each other for nearly eight decades. In the contest for Mediterranean sovereignty, both sides performed fantastic feats. Rome built a navy in two months, Hannibal's army scaled the thirteen-thousand-foot Alps, and Rome learned how to turn war elephants around to pulverize their masters.

The name "Punic Wars" comes from the Latin word *Punicus*, meaning Phoenician, a Semitic-speaking, seafaring people from Lebanon's coast. The Phoenicians colonized Carthage in today's Tunisia in North Africa. Carthage grew incredibly prosperous through its sea trade and ruled an empire that skirted the lower Mediterranean for centuries. But in the mid-200s BCE, it grappled with Rome in a lethal struggle for dominance.

It all began with pirates. Nefarious mercenaries invaded Messana (today's Messina) in Sicily, six miles across the Strait of Messina from southern Italy. The Mamertines plundered ships passing through the strait and raided the fields and cities of eastern Sicily for two decades. Finally, Hiero II, the ruler of Syracuse, decided to end

---

[28] Virgil, *The Aeneid, Book IV*, trans. A. S. Kline (Poetry in Translation, 2002). https://www.poetryintranslation.com/PITBR/Latin/VirgilAeneidIV.php.

their pillaging. He marched one hundred miles north to Messana, but the Mamertines allied with Carthage, which had a nearby fleet, and Hiero backed off.

To the pirates' dismay, Carthage stationed troops at Messana, cracking down on their plundering. The Mamertines decided to seek Rome's protection from Syracuse and kick out Carthage's garrison. Although hesitant to get involved with buccaneers, Rome was eager to impede Carthage's expanding control over Sicily. So, in 264 BCE, the Romans allied with the Mamertines and sent two legions to Sicily in their first military campaign off Italy's shores.

Apprehensive at this turn of events, Hiero turned to Carthage for help with Rome and the pirates. The first order of business for the Carthaginian commander Hanno was to crucify the garrison captain who had abandoned Messana without orders. Hanno then sailed his fleet to Messana before the Roman legions crossed the strait. The Roman legions sailed over at night, catching the Carthaginians and Syracusans by surprise and defeating their dual forces. The Romans then sailed down the channel to Syracuse, but Hiero immediately surrendered, brokering a deal where he allied with Rome to keep his position as Syracuse's ruler.

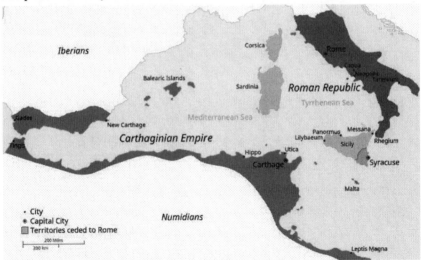

At the beginning of the First Punic War, Rome's only territory was Italy, while Carthage's empire covered Africa's northern coast and southern Spain.

In 262 BCE, the Roman forces in Sicily swelled to four legions led by both consuls. They conquered Carthage's ally Akragas on Sicily's southeastern coast and enslaved the citizens, prompting other Sicilian cities to defect to Rome rather than face its wrath. At this point, Rome realized that taking on Carthage, the world's supreme naval power, required warships, which it built at breakneck speed.

While the crews built one hundred quinqueremes and twenty smaller triremes, the future sailors practiced rowing in unison. The Romans knew their inexperience would put them at a disadvantage with Carthage's seasoned naval maneuvers. To put their close-contact combat skills into play, the Romans developed thirty-six-foot-long gangplanks to hook on the adversaries' ships so they could board and fight man to man. They also carried their catapults on board to shoot flaming missiles.

To Carthage's shock, Rome's neophyte navy won stunning victories in the Battle of Mylae and the Battle of Sulci. The Romans built over a hundred more ships and a naval force of fourteen thousand marines within two years. In what some consider history's largest naval battle—the Battle of Cape Ecnomus—they fought Carthage's navy off Sicily's coast. There were 680 ships and 300,000 men between the two navies. After a prolonged, bizarre day of fighting, Rome triumphed over Carthage, sinking or capturing ninety-four ships compared to twenty-four of their own. Carthage lost at least thirty thousand men.

Rome took the war to Africa, winning a land battle only ten miles from Carthage. But the Carthaginians allied with the Spartans and launched a counterattack, overwhelming the Romans with one hundred war elephants and a cavalry unit of four thousand. They butchered twelve thousand Romans; only two thousand escaped to be picked up by a fleet arriving from Rome. Another apocalypse awaited them, as a savage cyclone sunk 320 of their 400 ships, drowning 100,000 sailors in one of the world's deadliest shipwrecks of all time.

But the unstoppable Romans regrouped in Sicily, conquering Palermo and enslaving most of the population. They triumphed over Carthage in two more battles in 251 and 250 BCE, sending their captured elephants to Rome for the citizens' amusement.

However, another brutal storm sunk 150 ships on the way back from the war in Africa. Then, the Romans suffered a degrading loss when Carthage captured ninety-three more vessels.

That last fiasco was all Consul Pulcher's fault. He consulted his sacred chickens for an omen regarding his planned surprise attack on Carthage. But the chickens refused to eat, implying his plans were doomed. Unwilling to accept the omen, Pulcher thundered, "If you won't eat, you'll drink!"

He tossed the chickens, squawking and flapping, into the sea. After his ignominious naval disaster, Rome recalled him, where he stood trial on charges of impiety for drowning the sacred chickens. A sudden rainstorm interrupted the proceedings, and the magistrates never rescheduled. Yet, the Fates had their way, as Pulcher died soon after.[29]

Carthage's new admiral, Hamilcar Barca ("lightning"), plundered Italy's coastal towns and launched guerrilla attacks on Sicily. But Rome quickly built more ships and crushed Carthage's naval force. Carthage finally surrendered in 241 BCE, paying thirty-two hundred silver talents and turning Sicily over to Rome—its first offshore territory. The Romans quickly acquired the island of Sardinia, which threw off its Carthaginian overlords at the end of the First Punic War.

---

[29] Paul Sheridan, "The Sacred Chickens of Rome," *Anecdotes from Antiquity* (November 8th, 2015). http://www.anecdotesfromantiquity.net/the-sacred-chickens-of-rome.

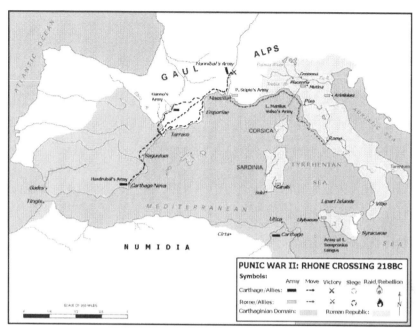

When the Second Punic War began, Carthage controlled part of North Africa's coast and most of Spain. Rome controlled Italy and the islands of Sicily, Sardinia, and Corsica.

The Second Punic War began in Iberia (Spain), where Carthage had colonies for centuries. After the First Punic War, Hamilcar Barca expanded Carthage's control from the coastal region to most of modern-day Spain. This enriched Carthage, helping it recover economically and renew its military resources. In 221 BCE, Carthage's army appointed Hamilcar's son, Hannibal, as their commander in chief, seeing his father's fire in his eyes.

Some Spanish cities resisted Carthage, including Saguntum, a trade ally with Rome. They had been messaging Rome about Hannibal's growing power, but Rome was distracted by the Macedonians. Hannibal attacked Saguntum in 219 BCE, taking the city and killing every adult. This atrocity triggered Rome's declaration of war on Carthage, beginning the Second Punic War. General Scipio Africanus sailed to Spain with sixty warships, but Hannibal had disappeared!

Leading ninety thousand soldiers, twelve thousand horsemen, and thirty-seven war elephants, Hannibal had marched up Spain's coast and scaled the 11,000-foot Pyrenees Mountains. After doing that, he was in Gaul (France) and headed toward the Alps. Receiving word that the Gauls were planning an attack on the opposite side of the Rhone River, Hannibal's lieutenant, Hanno, led a contingent of troops twenty-five miles upstream. They crossed the river and stealthily crept toward the Gauls' camp.

The Gauls were utterly fixated on Hannibal's army on the opposite side of the river, especially the elephants, which they'd never seen. They watched as Hannibal loaded his army, horses, and animals on boats and rafts, ready to attack the Carthaginians as soon as they were within range of their arrows and spears. At that moment, Hanno led a surprise attack from their rear, overwhelming and scattering them to the hills.

The thirteen-thousand-foot Isère Alps lay between France and Italy, and the Carthaginians had to get across before the December snows. They clawed their way up the steep pass with their horses and elephants, dodging boulders thrown from above by the menacing mountain people. They left their assailants behind on their downward trek, but the terrain was terrifying, with constricted, ice-slick paths and deep snow. Occasionally, someone would lose their footing and freefall a mile to the jagged stones below.

Then, the Carthaginians turned a bend to find a landslide covering the path; the deep snow prevented them from moving further. The soldiers laboriously removed the rocks so the horses, mules, and elephants could cross. The horses and mules clambered over first, trotting down to the tree line, where they finally found grass. But the famished elephants had to wait three more days before the path was safe enough for them to maneuver.

Hannibal's brutal trek over the Alps gave him the element of surprise.
PMRMaeyaert, CC BY-SA 4.0 <https://creativecommons.org/licenses/by-sa/4.0>, via Wikimedia Commons; https://commons.wikimedia.org/wiki/File:PM_110453_Liebig_Chromos.jpg

Hannibal lost two-thirds of his army, half his cavalry, and an unknown number of elephants in the confrontations with the Gauls and in the dangerous passage over the Alps.[30] But as he descended into Italy, the Gauls there, who had immigrated centuries earlier and sacked Rome in 390 BCE, quickly joined forces with him. The Romans thought Hannibal was somewhere in Spain or France; he caught them off-guard when he suddenly showed up at their northern border.

Hannibal wreaked havoc, pursuing a scorched-earth strategy through Italy, destroying crops and other resources. In the 217 BCE Battle at Lake Trasimene in central Italy, he killed or captured twenty-five thousand men. Rome had the numerical advantage, but Hannibal had ingenious tactics and an indomitable spirit. In the 216 BCE Battle of Cannae in southern Italy, he killed 50,000 Romans, losing only 5,700 of his own. While central Italy staunchly supported Rome, Italy's southern city-states defected to Carthage.

Rome finally rallied, cutting off the Carthaginians' supplies and manpower that were coming into Italy. General Scipio was still in Iberia and racked up an astounding triumph in 209 BCE by taking control of Carthage's supply network and treasury. The ecstatic Romans elected Scipio as their new consul. Africa became his next

---

[30] Polybius, *Histories, Book III.*

target. With 440 ships, he sailed to Carthage and attacked in the middle of the night, dividing his forces and pouncing on the Carthaginians from both sides.

After Carthage's loss, its Numidian Berber allies switched sides to Rome. Scipio's cavalry had outmaneuvered the Numidians' expert horsemen, and they wanted to be on the winning side. In the concluding Battle of Zama, Hannibal rushed back to Africa in 202 BCE to defend Carthage from Scipio. The Romans outnumbered the Carthaginians, although they still put up a ferocious defense.

Eighty war elephants decided the battle. Hannibal sent them in an onslaught toward the Romans, but Scipio was experienced with elephants by this time. He ordered his men to step aside, allowing the elephants to charge through to the back of the Roman lines. The Romans surrounded the creatures with their spears and sent them toward the Carthaginians in a counterstrike. While the Carthaginians were busy getting out of the elephants' way, the Roman and Berber cavalry swooped around to Hannibal's rearguard. They trapped his forces against the Roman infantry, with the elephants creating chaos in the middle.

The day ended with a spectacular victory for Rome, with Carthage losing twenty thousand men to Rome's five thousand. Carthage surrendered, ending the Second Punic War by disbanding its navy and agreeing not to fight anyone without Rome's permission. Carthage kept their North African territories, except for Numidia, but lost Spain and other offshore holdings. It paid two hundred gold talents for Rome's war expenses and annual tribute for the next fifty years.

Hannibal remained in Carthage as chief magistrate and attempted to reform the city's political system. He established direct elections of officials and term limits and eliminated the misuse of state funds. But Hannibal's reform efforts earned him enemies in Carthage. When Rome became suspicious that Hannibal was colluding with the Seleucid Empire, Hannibal decided to leave town and spent the rest of his life in Asia. For the next five decades, Carthage kept its treaty and paid tribute to Rome. Carthage provided barley and grain and even allied with Rome on occasional military expeditions. But trouble loomed ahead for the two great cities.

Chapter 8: The Third Punic War and the Fall of Carthage

"It's not fair! We can't defend ourselves!" the Carthaginians wailed in desperation.

Numidia (today's Algeria and western Libya) surrounded Carthage to the west and south and was an ally of Rome. Numidia's King Masinissa took advantage of this alliance to invade Carthage's territory, steadily chipping away until Carthage's lands decreased by half. Carthage was frustratingly helpless to do anything. The treaty with Rome stipulated it couldn't fight anyone without Rome's permission. But Rome, which was secretly pleased that their one-time greatest rival was rapidly losing territory, wouldn't permit Cartage to fight a Roman ally.

Finally, the desperate Carthaginians could no longer restrain themselves. If they didn't do something, they would lose everything! When King Masinissa brazenly attacked the Carthaginian city of Oroscopa, Carthage mustered thirty-one thousand troops to defend their territory. But after fifty years, Carthage had fallen out of practice in the art of war. They underestimated their enemy, assuming the Numidians were an undisciplined desert tribe when Masinissa had formed a regimented force with sensational tactics and logistics.

Masinissa slyly moved the battle to rugged desert terrain, where there was little water or food. Eventually, the starving, dehydrated Carthaginian army surrendered. But the Numidians ignored their surrender and massacred them. Carthage's warriors never left their borders; they were only defending themselves against Numidia. Even then, they failed wretchedly. But they didn't ask or receive permission from Rome. So, technically, they had broken their treaty.

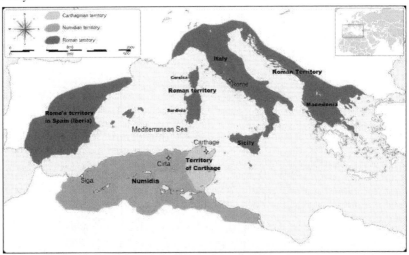

Rome controlled most of the upper Mediterranean, and Numidia surrounded Carthage at the beginning of the Third Punic War.

"Carthago delendam est!" Cato cried out. "Carthage must be destroyed!"

Two years earlier, the ancient Cato the Elder had visited Carthage with some fellow senators to sort out the problems with Numidia. Cato was astounded at Carthage's staggering wealth. Carthage had always been a vital trade center. Now that it no longer funded a navy and wasn't spending a fortune on military campaigns, it had recouped its former splendor. To Cato, Carthage's conspicuous prosperity presented a tremendous threat to Rome.

It wasn't that Carthage had done anything terrible. Rome received its annual tribute like clockwork, and Carthage had shown nothing but respect to Rome. It wasn't what Carthage had done; it was what it could do with such vast wealth, like build or buy a naval fleet and hire a legion of mercenary warriors. And so, the octogenarian Cato ended every speech in the Senate with "Carthago delenda est! Carthage must be destroyed!"

The younger senators, those born after the Second Punic War had ended, smirked and rolled their eyes when the veteran of the Second Punic War ranted. Carthage had no navy, and its army was a joke. It presented no threat to Rome. And anyway, a little fear was good for the republic: it kept everyone on their toes. The younger senators nodded vigorously when Corculum, Scipio Africanus's son-in-law, responded to Cato by ending his speeches with "Carthago servanda est! Carthage must be saved!"

But Cato's fear-mongering began stirring the Roman concept of a "just war." For the Romans, justification for war included more than defending the republic against attack. It could also include perceived slights to Roman prestige. Since Carthage's surrender during the Second Punic War, it had not posed a threat to Rome or anyone else. But Cato regularly stirred up fear in the Romans' minds, despite all the evidence to the contrary. Rumors circulated that Carthage was cutting timber to build a new naval fleet. The Carthaginians were cutting trees but for building merchant ships, not war vessels.[31]

And now, it seemed like Cato's dire predictions were coming true. Carthage had dared to go to war without permission! They breached the treaty and attacked an ally! It did not matter that they had acted in self-defense and suffered a horrendous loss. Their insubordination and military action against a Roman ally insulted Rome's honor and prestige. Something had to be done.

Carthage sent its ambassadors to Rome to explain what happened: they'd only fought in self-defense and lost most of their army in the debacle. But Rome had already decided it had cause for a just war. They shot back at the Carthaginians, "Send us three hundred children from your nobility as hostages, and maybe then we'll consider peace terms."

---

[31] Robert J. Kane, "The Third Punic War: An Intelligence Failure from Antiquity," *American Intelligence Journal* 36, no. 1 (2019): 162–63. https://www.jstor.org/stable/27066349.

The ambassadors took the news home to the distraught people, who moaned, "How could we give up three hundred of our children? Who knows what the Romans would do to them!"

But in anguish, they surrendered three hundred of their sons to Rome. Would they ever see them again? And would it even help? The Romans' stipulations only grew. In 149 BCE, Rome sent eighty thousand soldiers and four thousand cavalry units to Africa, demanding Carthage's unconditional surrender. "You must shut down your army, recall your military, and turn over all your weapons."

The Carthaginians fumed, "They can't seriously think we'll give up our army and disarm! How would we protect ourselves?"

But just as they had handed over their children, they relinquished their weapons. They turned over 200,000 sets of chainmail armor and 2,000 catapults. Then came the Romans' final ultimatum: "Oh, one more thing: leave Carthage. You can resettle inland, but you must be at least ten miles from the coast."

When the envoys brought the news back to Carthage, the citizens raged. "Leave Carthage? This has been our home for a thousand years! We'd lose our harbor; how would we pursue trade? We'd end up poverty-stricken! Our walls protect us here. Would we settle inland? In the desert? With no protection from the Berbers? How could we possibly survive?"

The Carthaginians refused, and Rome's legions headed to Carthage, starting the Third Punic War. The city of Carthage lay on a piece of land that jutted out into the Gulf of Tunis, protected to the south by the Lake of Tunis. A twenty-three-mile wall encircled the city. The three miles of the brick wall facing the mainland was forty-two feet high and thirty feet thick. In front of the wall was a seventy-foot-wide ditch. No army ever penetrated that stretch of wall. The Romans tried but gave up at the beginning of the Third Punic War. Instead, they focused on cutting off the supply lines between Carthage and its allies.

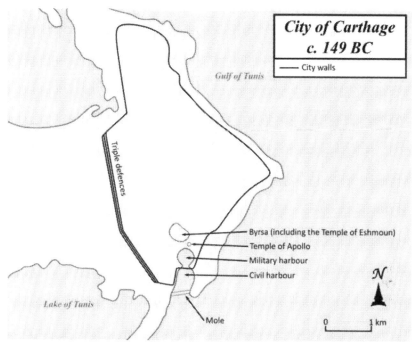

City of Carthage
c. 149 BC

City walls

Gulf of Tunis

Triple defences

Byrsa (including the Temple of Eshmoun)
Temple of Apollo
Military harbour
Civil harbour

Lake of Tunis

Mole

N

0   1 km

Carthage was on an isthmus with impenetrable triple walls facing the mainland.
Harrias, CC BY-SA 4.0 <https://creativecommons.org/licenses/by-sa/4.0>, via Wikimedia Commons; https://commons.wikimedia.org/wiki/File:City_of_Carthage_circa_149_BC.png

Most of our information on the Third Punic War comes from the Greek historian Polybius. He was also a hostage, among about a thousand that Rome demanded from the recently conquered Achaean League. He arrived in Italy from Greece at the same time as the child hostages from Carthage.[32] Polybius became friends with Scipio Aemilianus, the adopted grandson of Scipio Africanus, the hero of the Second Punic War. After being released from his captivity, Polybius accompanied Scipio to Africa, interviewing both the Romans and Carthaginians as he recorded the war's history.

The siege of Carthage lasted almost three years. Carthage released any slaves willing to fight for the city and amassed a twenty-thousand-man army. To the Romans' surprise, the Carthaginians had either not relinquished all their weapons or reaccumulated some of them. Led by General Hasdrubal, the Carthaginians disrupted the Roman supply lines and attacked smaller bands of

---

[32] Polybius, *Histories, Book 36.*

Romans foraging in the agricultural regions around the city.

The Roman army was divided into two contingents, each with a specific assignment. One legion was to fill the ditch in front of the great wall so that they could scale it. The other group was to approach the smaller wall facing the lake and put ladders up from their ships to scale the walls. Both attempts failed. The next plan was to fill in Lake Tunis's shoreline just next to the walls so they could roll their siege engines close to them. They constructed two battering rams and managed to break down part of the wall facing the Lake of Tunis, but the Carthaginians fought fiercely, driving the Romans away from the breach. That night, they snuck out of the city and burned many of the Roman siege engines.

The Carthaginians received a welcome lull when the Roman contingent at the Lake of Tunis fell ill due to the mosquito-ridden swampland, the July heat, and inadequate clean drinking water. The commander decided to move his men away from the marsh to the gulf side, where there was more fresh air and fewer insects. Once the men had recovered, they began focusing on Carthage's harbor. Carthage had a protected port for its merchant ships. Its warships passed through the first harbor to a second, more secure circular harbor.

Carthage had a harbor for merchant ships (lower left) and a round interior port for military ships accessed through the first harbor.

Despite the Romans' vigilance, supply ships from Carthage's Phoenician allies continually managed to elude the blockade. The Phoenicians had been seafaring people for almost two millennia; they were perhaps the world's first long-distance seafarers. Their ships were faster than the Romans' and could maneuver more easily. With their superior marine skills, Carthage still received regular shipments of food, weapons, and other necessities.

Moving the Roman camp placed them closer to Carthage's harbor, which they first considered an advantage because they could monitor any ships trying to enter or leave. But the intrepid Carthaginians used fireships against them. These were older ships near the end of their lifespan, which they would fill with brush and cover with tar. They would sail out into the harbor, set the ships on fire, and quickly jump off. They launched the fireships in coordination with the wind and tide so that they would sail straight toward the Roman fleet, crashing into their ships and setting them on fire. The Carthaginians swiftly decimated the Roman fleet by using this tactic.

What Rome had expected to be a swift victory was morphing into a prolonged siege in which they could not seem to gain any advantage. What's worse, the other Phoenician cities on Africa's coast, except for Utica, refused to submit, as did the smaller towns in Carthage's territory. To top it off, one of the Numidian tribes, led by its king, Bithyas, defected to Carthage, sending eight hundred cavalry units to fight the Romans. By this point, King Masinissa of Numidia had died. His two sons assured Rome they'd send money and weapons, but they did not follow through. They seemed to be waiting to see how events played out in the struggle between Rome and Carthage.[33]

Back in Rome, the senators were livid that affairs were still dragging out in Carthage. It was time for the elections of new consuls for the typical one-year term. The public demanded Scipio Aemilianus be elected, even though he was younger than the age requirement of forty-one. He was the grandson of Scipio Africanus, who many considered to be the most stellar military commander in

[33]Appian. *Punic Wars.*
http://www.perseus.tufts.edu/hopper/text?doc=Perseus%3Atext%3A1999.01.0230%3Atext%3DPun.%3Achapter%3D16%3Asection%3D111.

history. After all, he was the general who defeated Hannibal and ended the Second Punic War.

After being elected and dispatched to Carthage, Scipio Aemilianus wasted no time dealing with the issues that had stymied his predecessors. He built a causeway across the entrance to Carthage's harbor, preventing any ships from coming or going. Out of sight in the military port, the Carthaginians were surreptitiously building fifty new ships. When they finished construction, they broke through their own wall to open a new harbor entrance. The fifty vessels sailed out to confront the Roman fleet. Due to the Carthaginians' advantage of surprise, the battle was in their favor until they tried to reenter their new narrow harbor entrance at the end of the day. They quickly clogged the small entrance, and the prevailing current pushed many of them against the sea wall, damaging the ships beyond repair or leaving them vulnerable to the Romans.

Scipio Aemilianus's catapults flung boulders against the walls, and the battering ramps slammed them, but the walls did not budge. He focused on the walls along the harbor, which weren't as thick as those facing the mainland. The Carthaginians snuck out at night, swimming across the harbor to set fire to the siege engines, but the Romans would quickly repair or rebuild them. The Romans also controlled the new entrance into the port, preventing supplies and food from coming in.

In the spring of 146 BCE, the Romans finally got inside the city. In a nighttime attack, some younger soldiers climbed a brick tower that the Romans had spent months building near the wall. They threw a long gangplank over to the walls. Once inside the city, they opened the gates for the Roman army, and four thousand soldiers poured in. The people inside were disoriented and panicked at the soldiers' loud shouts, but they spilled into the streets with whatever weapons they had to defend their city.

The Romans worked their way through Carthage for six days and nights, taking each street and house until all the citizens had either escaped, been hewed down, or perished in the buildings as they burned. Exhausted, Scipio Aemilianus climbed up a high bluff to watch the ancient city reduced to ashes. He wept as he remembered Carthage's vast empire, astounding wealth, massive fleets, and elephants. He honored the bravery with which the Carthaginians had defended their city for three years, only for it to end in the city's total destruction. He reflected on the rise and fall of his ancestral Troy and wept again as he prophesied Rome's fall in the future. Carthage's destruction was complete. Never again would the Carthaginians thrive and rule the waves from their glittering city. With all competition obliterated, Rome now had total power over the western Mediterranean.

PART THREE: Consequence and Legacy (120–40 BCE)

Chapter 9: The Gallic Wars

"Sir! We have news! The Helvetii are on the move!"

Julius Caesar swung around. "The Helvetii? I thought they abandoned their plan to migrate. Where are they heading?"

"Straight toward us, sir! They plan to cross the bridge at Geneva."

"Well then, we'll have to assemble the troops and march on the double to Geneva!"

"Yes, sir. And I'm sorry this is happening just after you got here."

"Oh, don't be sorry." Caesar grinned. "This fits my agenda perfectly."

Julius Caesar, the descendent of an ancient aristocratic Roman family, was a statesman, a warrior, and a writer. While fighting in Gaul (France and parts of Belgium, western Germany, and northern Italy), he wrote an eight-volume account of his experiences in the Gallic Wars.[34] As he finished each book, he sent it back to Italy, keeping Rome abreast of his campaign with a coherent narrative of his victories over the immense territory.[35]

---

[34] Julius Caesar, *The Gallic Wars*, trans. W. A. McDevitte and W. S. Bohn (The Internet Classics Archive). http://classics.mit.edu/Caesar/gallic.1.1.html.

[35] Josiah Osgood, "The Pen and the Sword: Writing and Conquest in Caesar's Gaul," *Classical Antiquity* 28, no. 2 (2009): 328. https://doi.org/10.1525/ca.2009.28.2.328.

Pliny reported that Caesar was an avid multitasker, with at least one slave always by his side as his secretary who quickly transcribed Caesar's rapid-fire dictations. As Caesar heard or read reports from the battlefield or letters from Rome, he would dictate several letters at once to various recipients. He would travel around in his sedan chair to inspect camps, garrisons, and cities, with his slave always by his side, taking dictation.

In 59 BCE, Caesar became one of Rome's two consuls, with Bibulus as the other. Bibulus was literally the victim of dirty politics, as Caesar organized his cronies to fling him to the ground and pour excrement over him when he attempted to block a bill. Humiliated, Bibulus remained at home for the rest of the year as a puppet consul while Caesar swung the senators' votes. At the end of his one-year consulship, the Senate appointed Caesar to a five-year term as proconsul and governor of Cisalpine Gaul and Transalpine Gaul.

Sculpture of Julius Caesar by Andrea di Pietro di Marco Ferrucci, circa 1512.
Metropolitan Museum of Art, CC0, via Wikimedia Commons;
https://commons.wikimedia.org/wiki/File:Julius_Caesar_MET_267739.jpg

Cisalpine Gaul was the northernmost region of Italy. Cisalpine means "this side of the Alps." Centuries earlier, the Celts crossed the Alps into Italy and sacked Rome in 390 BCE, but the Italians eventually forced them back into northern Italy. Transalpine Gaul, on the other side of the Alps in today's southeastern France, became a Roman province in 118 BCE. By this point, the Celts of Gaul were building cities and becoming affluent through trade with Rome. But they were still ferocious and powerful warriors with sharp fighting skills and towering physiques.

At the end of a consul's term, he could face prosecution for abusing the powers of his office. Caesar had bent a few rules and abused his co-consul, so finagling a governorship abroad kept him immune from prosecution. Victorious military campaigns would ramp up his prestige and build his political power, not to mention enriching him through the plunders of war. Caesar headed to Gaul with four legions, veterans he had already led into battle as the governor of Hispania three years earlier.

In his *Gallic Wars*, Caesar describes three main tribal confederations in Gaul: the northern Belgae, the southwestern Aquitani, and the Celtic Gauls in central Transalpine Gaul. He said each tribal group had its own language and distinctive culture. In Caesar's opinion, the Belgae were the bravest of the three because they were remote from civilization and things that "tend to effeminate the mind." They were also in constant warfare with the Germans, which kept them in excellent fighting shape. A fourth group was the Celtic Helvetii, who had been forced out of southern Germany by the Teutonic Germans into today's northern Switzerland.

The regions of Gaul in Julius Caesar's day.

The Greek historian Posidonius described the Helvetii as peaceable people who became affluent through prospecting for gold in the rivers. Several years earlier, one of their noblemen, Orgetorix, convinced many of the Helvetii that they should migrate into Gaul and establish a kingdom on the coast. At that point, the Helvetii were a confederation ruled by local leaders, but Orgetorix wanted to unite all the tribes with himself as king. The tribal magistrates squelched the idea, and Orgetorix died, apparently of suicide.

When the Romans heard this news, they thought the situation was resolved. However, in March 58 BCE, just as Julius Caesar assumed the governorship of Gaul, the Helvetii burned down their homes and farmlands in about twelve towns and four hundred villages. Caesar said that 368,000 Helvetii began trekking west, carrying provisions for three months. Several neighboring tribes joined them, also destroying their homes before leaving.

The best route for their trek toward the Atlantic coast was right through the Roman section of Gaul. They headed for the town of Geneva, where a bridge covered the Rhone River. The Allobroges people of Geneva had no strong ties to the Romans, and the Helvetii thought they might let them cross. If not, they would force their way over the bridge. But Caesar's legion got there first and ordered the Genevans to break down the bridge.

The Helvetii sent their ambassadors to Caesar. They told him, "Sir, we intend to march through your province without harming it in any way. This is the only way to our destination. Please give your consent."

But Caesar remembered an incident five decades earlier when he was just a child. The Tigurini tribe, part of the Helvetii confederation, was on a raiding spree through Gaul. The consul at the time, Lucius Cassius Longinus, had chased them to the Atlantic Ocean, but the Tigurini ambushed and killed him and ten thousand of his legionaries. The Tigurini forced the surviving Romans to "pass under the yoke" of spears, a ritual humiliation.[36]

Caesar leaned back and rubbed his chin. He doubted the Helvetii would pass through his province without stirring up trouble and didn't intend to grant their request. But he needed time for the rest of his soldiers to arrive. "I need a few days to consider your request. Come back on the Ides of April, and I'll give you my answer then."

In the next two weeks, Caesar put his men to work building a sixteen-foot high and eighteen-mile-long wall along Lake Geneva. He appointed garrisons and guard stations all along the Rhone River to prevent the Helvetii from crossing. When the Helvetii returned for his answer, he told them they could not cross. They tried to pass over by boat or by fording a shallow part of the river, but the Romans were alert and stymied their attempts.

The Helvetii negotiated an alternative route through the Sequani tribe's territory. The Helvetii and Sequani exchanged hostages, pledging that the Helvetii would have safe passage if they respected

---

[36] Caesar, *The Gallic Wars*, Book 1, Chapter 7.

the Sequani territory. Caesar caught up with them just as they were crossing the slow-flowing Saône River. All but about one-fourth had crossed, and Caesar massacred the ones left behind, then built a pontoon bridge and crossed over. He hunted down the Helvetii and fought them in the horrendous Battle of Bibracte, reportedly killing two-thirds of the Helvetii.

Caesar's next challenge was the Germanic Suebi tribe, which was pouring across the Rhine River into Gaul. By this point, Caesar had returned briefly to Italy to round up two more legions, giving him six legions in Gaul. He met the Suebi army and put them to flight, killing most of their soldiers and chasing the remnants back across the river; they would never challenge Rome again. Caesar's victories against the Helvetii and Suebi prompted many Gallic tribes to ally with Rome. He dealt with Belgae raiders (from today's Belgium) by circumnavigating them and attacking their primary city. The Belgae snuck back into their town by night but were unprepared for a Roman siege and quickly surrendered.

An embarrassing setback faced Caesar in the Battle of the Sabis with the Nervii, another Belgic tribe. With sixty thousand men, the Nervii launched a surprise attack on the Romans as they set up camp. Two of Caesar's legions were still nine miles away. The Romans put their military discipline into play against the more disorganized Nervii, driving part of the Nervii back across the river. But the remaining Nervii outflanked the Romans' right wing and captured the unguarded Roman camp. Caesar jumped into the front lines himself to fight the onslaught. Caesar's two remaining legions showed up just in the nick of time to turn the tide of the battle and send the remaining Nervii packing.

In 56 BCE, the Roman forces collided with the seafaring Veneti of the northern Brittany peninsula when the Veneti imprisoned the Roman officers who came to collect grain requisitions. The Romans had little experience in the rough Atlantic Ocean, but Caesar set his men to work building ships to take on the Veneti in a naval battle. That did not go well for the Romans, as the Veneti had superior seamanship skills and could easily outmaneuver them.

Rome finally prevailed in the Battle of Morbihan, as better weather enabled them to employ the naval skills they'd perfected in the Punic Wars. They used grappling hooks to destroy the Venetis' sails and rigging and pull their ships close enough to slap their gangplank on the enemy's ships to board them. Then, the Romans exercised their superior combat skills, fighting man to man, and destroyed the Veneti fleet.

While Caesar was fighting at sea, his generals, Crassus and Sabinus, confronted Normandy and Aquitania. Sabinus easily defeated the coalition tribes of Normandy by forcing them to approach his army on a grueling uphill climb. They were too tired to fight when they reached the top. Crassus faced more difficulties in Aquitania, as these tribes had previously allied with the Romans and knew their strategies and tricks. Crassus finally launched a surprise rear attack on their camp, which was only fortified at the front. The ensuing victory brought southwest Gaul to the Roman Republic. At the end of 56 BCE, the Senate awarded Caesar another five years of governing Gaul.

In 55 BCE, Caesar pulled two attention-getting feats to build prestige back in Rome: crossing the Rhine and crossing the English Channel to Britain. The Rhine divided Germany from Gaul, and once again, the Germanic tribes were forcing the Celts out of Germany and into Gaul. The initial battle ended with the Celts defeating the Roman Gallic allies, despite being outnumbered five to one. Embarrassed, Caesar attacked their undefended base camp and massacred thousands of women and children, compelling Rome's Senate to prosecute him for war crimes. Prosecution was futile, given that Caesar was immune as long as he served as Gaul's governor. Caesar then launched an eighteen-day raid in Germany, building a timber bridge over the Rhine and burning the bridge behind him on his return.

Caesar crossed the English Channel to Britain in August with two legions, but the Britons were lined up on the shore awaiting him. He tried sailing up the coast, but they followed. Finally, the standard-bearer led the way by jumping in the sea and wading ashore to plant the Roman standard on Britain's shore. The Roman soldiers quickly waded after him to protect the standard. After a short, indecisive battle, the Romans returned to Gaul for the winter.

Caesar spent the winter devising a more organized assault on Britain, crossing the channel in 54 BCE with five legions and two thousand cavalry units. Rather than facing the Romans in open battle, the Britons launched guerilla raids with their chariots and horses, skillfully outmaneuvering the Roman cavalry. They attacked a small Roman contingent, expecting an easy win. But to their surprise, the Romans formed ranks and soundly defeated them, taking the wind out of the Britons' sails. Although the Briton tribes had previously fought each other, they united under the warlord Cassivellaunus, Caesar defeated Cassivellaunus, and the Briton tribes surrendered, agreeing to pay an annual tribute.

At this point, Caesar received news of mayhem in Gaul. Many tribes had revolted against Rome and ambushed General Sabine, killing most of his army. Caesar immediately sailed back from Britain with two legions to rescue General Cicero but not before Cicero lost 90 percent of his legion. Unrest continued among the conquered tribes until war finally exploded in 52 BCE. The conflict had been instigated by druid priests, and the people were united under King Vercingetorix of the Arverni tribe.

The revolt culminated with the Romans laying siege to the town of Alesia in Burgundy, where Vercingetorix had amassed a hundred thousand troops. The Celtic king planned to trap Caesar's forces between Alesia's walls and another Celtic army that was on its way to the region. But he never expected the extent of Caesar's siegeworks: twenty-five miles of trenches, towers, and hidden snares. And yes, Caesar *did* anticipate the Gauls launching a rear attack and was well prepared, pulverizing the rebellion. Vercingetorix and most of the Gallic tribes surrendered, except for holdouts in southwestern Gaul positioned in the hill fort of Uxellodunum. The Romans dug tunnels to the spring supplying water to the citadel, cutting off their water supply. When the rebels surrendered, Caesar cut off their hands.

By 50 BCE, Rome held control over all of Gaul only eight years after Caesar assumed its governorship. Rome would rule Gaul for almost five centuries, and the Old French language would rise out of Roman Latin. Caesar had grown in political prestige and wealth through the process. He was poised to turn Roman politics upside down, becoming Rome's first long-term dictator, which was the beginning of the end for the republic.

Chapter 10: Caesar and Pompey: Triumvirates and Civil War

"It's absolutely absurd, Caesar!" Pompey growled. "My men have been fighting nonstop in Asia! We've conquered nine hundred cities, captured eight hundred pirate ships, and won massive provinces for Rome! All I'm asking is a small plot of farmland for each of my soldiers so that they can support their families. And I need the Senate to honor the treaties I made with the new provinces. Can you believe those idiots in the Senate are opposing the bill? They all own vast estates but are refusing my men a patch of land in the eastern regions they've conquered!"

"I know, I know, my friend," Caesar soothed. "The senators are incompetent fools only interested in retaining their wealth and power."

The two men sipped their wine silently for a few minutes as Caesar looked speculatively at Pompey. "You know," he said softly, "there's a way around your impasse."

Pompey's eyebrow lifted. "Keep talking!"

"A triumvirate. You're a popular war hero. I've got influential connections in the Senate, and I'm the high priest of the College of Pontiffs. You get me elected as consul, and I'll pass your land bill!"

Pompey frowned. "But you said a triumvirate. Who's the third person?"

Caesar chose his words carefully. "Well, we need money to sway the votes. And I haven't any; I'm deep in debt."

Pompey nodded. "I haven't that kind of money either. So, who's going to be our financier? Oh, you can't possibly mean Crassus? I loathe the man!"

Caesar leaned forward. "You don't have to like Crassus or have much to do with him. You're manipulating things behind the scenes. I champion your bill, and Crassus swings the votes with his money. What do you say?"

Pompey smiled. "I say I need a wife!"

Caesar looked confused for a moment. "Ah! You mean Julia! You want to marry Julia?"

Pompey reddened. "I do. I know I'm much older, but I'm ready to settle down now. Your daughter is beautiful, kind, and conscientious. Quite frankly, I'm infatuated with her!"

Caesar grinned. "All right, my friend. Julia shall be your bride!"

And so, the "Gang of Three," which would upend Roman politics, was formed.

Crassus, Pompey, and Caesar, the three men who formed the First Triumvirate, were all previously connected to a civil war between the consul Lucius Sulla and his former military commander Gaius Marius. Marius, who was married to Julius Caesar's aunt Julia, had the distinction of serving as Rome's consul seven times, but between his sixth and seventh consulship, Sulla was elected consul. The former comrades-in-arms became bitter rivals.

After his election, Sulla immediately headed to Pontus to fight King Mithridates VI. No sooner had he left than his political enemies convinced the Senate to recall Sulla and send Marius to command the campaign instead. Receiving this news, an enraged Sulla marched back to Rome with five legions, reconsolidated his power, declared Marius a *hostis publicus* ("public enemy"), then returned to Pontus. Marius fled to Africa, but after Sulla left Rome, Marius slipped back to Italy with his army while Rome was in the throes of a civil war between the patricians and plebeians. He usurped control of Rome, murderously purging his political foes. In late 85 BCE, he was elected to his seventh term as consul. He took office on January 1st, 86 BCE, but suddenly died two weeks later.

Sulla wrapped up his campaign in Pontus and sailed back to Rome, retaking the city. The Senate appointed him dictator, which was customary during an emergency, but it was only meant to last a few months. Instead, Sulla ruled as dictator until shortly before his death, turning Rome into a bloodbath by executing everyone he considered a potential threat. He killed dozens each day, sometimes hundreds. In the power play between Marius and Sulla, Crassus's and Pompey's families supported Sulla, while Caesar's family supported Marius.

The slave trade, extortion, and land speculation made Crassus Rome's richest man.
Diagram Lajard, CC0, via Wikimedia Commons;
https://commons.wikimedia.org/wiki/File:Roman_bust_in_Ny_Carlsberg_Glyptotek,_crop.jpg

Marcus Licinius Crassus came from a respected plebeian family. Before Sulla regained control of Rome, Consul Cinna was executing or exiling Sulla's supporters, so Crassus had to get out of town quickly. He joined up with Sulla in Greece, where he fought alongside Pompey. Crassus won special distinction in a battle against the Marian forces, where he annihilated his foes and then asked Sulla if he needed help. Sulla was in trouble; his center forces were giving way before the enemy, so Crassus jumped in and saved the day.

Marius confiscated Crassus's family's property, so when the tables turned, Crassus gained back his fortune and more. He bought property expropriated from Sulla's enemies at scandalously low prices. Plutarch said he built his fabulous riches by "making the public calamities his greatest source of revenue." He established Rome's first fire brigade with five hundred firemen but only put out the fires if the owners agreed to sell the properties to him at rock bottom prices.[37] Estimates by Plutarch and Pliny place his wealth around what would be $13.7 billion today.

Despite Crassus's successful military career and enormous fortune, he couldn't compete with Pompey, who was building up a stellar reputation with his campaign in Hispania. Crassus's chance to gain fame came when Spartacus led the great slave revolt. Crassus offered to fund, train, and provide weapons for an army to defeat the slaves since Rome's legions were tied up in Hispania and Pontus.

The war against the runaway slaves dragged on for two years. In the meantime, Pompey returned from Hispania with his legions, flushed with victory. Rome appointed Pompey to deal with the slave crisis, but Crassus didn't want to share his glory. Propelled to end the revolt in a grand show of force before Pompey arrived in southern Italy, Crassus relentlessly chased down the escaped slaves. He killed most of them in battle or by crucifixion.

When Pompey was nominated to become Rome's consul in 70 BCE, Crassus swallowed his pride and asked for his support for his own nomination as co-consul. Pompey agreed, figuring that Crassus's immense prosperity made him a better friend than an enemy. Both men won the election; however, neither man trusted the other, and "their contentiousness rendered their consulship barren politically and without achievement."[38]

---

[37] Plutarch, *The Parallel Lives*, Volume III.

[38] Plutarch, *The Parallel Lives*, Volume III.

The renowned war hero Pompey joined forces with Caesar and Crassus.

Gnaeus Pompeius Magnus (better known as Pompey) came from the Picentes tribe on the far side of the Apennine Mountains from Rome. Pompey's father, Strabo, had risen through the ranks to become Rome's consul in 89 BCE but was struck by lightning two years later while defending Rome from Marius. When Sulla marched back to Rome to retake it in 84 BCE, Pompey raised three legions of his father's men to help defeat the Marians. Sulla persuaded Pompey to divorce his first wife and marry Sulla's stepdaughter, Aemilia. As it turned out, she was already pregnant with another man's child and died in childbirth soon after.

Pompey spent the next decade chasing down the remnants of the Marian rebels who had escaped and were attempting to establish strongholds in Sicily, North Africa, and Hispania. He crushed the rebellion of Rome's one-time general Sertorius, who had fallen in with pirates and led the Spanish tribes in fighting Roman forces in Hispania. After Pompey's skillful conquest, he marched over the Pyrenees into Gaul and then over the Alps into Italy, conquering 876 towns for Rome along the way.

In 66 BCE, Rome sent Pompey and eight legions east to deal with King Mithridates VI in Pontus, who once again attempted to overthrow Roman power in the Black Sea region. Overwhelmed and outnumbered, Mithridates fled his kingdom, unsuccessfully seeking asylum in Armenia with his son-in-law King Tigranes. He then hid out in the Crimean Peninsula in today's Ukraine, where he eventually committed suicide. Once Mithridates no longer presented a threat, Pompey organized Rome's new frontiers in eastern Europe and western Asia into provinces.

Next, Pompey marched to Syria, which had destabilized when the Seleucid Empire, which had once ruled most of the Middle East, had collapsed. Pompey conquered the major Syrian cities and turned Syria into a Roman province. He then headed south to Judea, which had been semi-autonomous since the 163 BCE Maccabean Revolt. Judea's two princes were immersed in a civil war after Aristobulus II stole his brother Hyrcanus II's throne and priesthood. In this era, the Jewish high priest was also the king. Antipater the Idumean, Hyrcanus's advisor, convinced Hyrcanus to ally with the Arabian king Aretas III and overthrow Aristobulus.

Pompey arrived just as the Arabians were laying siege to Jerusalem. He chased off the Arabs and attacked the heavily fortified temple where Aristobulus was hiding. Pompey broke down the temple walls but left the temple treasures in place, telling the priests to purify the temple and resume their sacrifices. He took Aristobulus back to Rome as a prisoner and restored Hyrcanus II as the high priest but not as king. Judea was now a Roman province, and Julius Caesar later appointed Antipater as the Roman procurator there. After Antipater's death, the Roman Senate appointed his son, Herod the Great, as Judea's vassal king. Herod was a bloodthirsty ruler and is remembered for his atrocities against his citizens and his own family.

Julius Caesar united Pompey and Crassus in the First Triumvirate.
https://commons.wikimedia.org/wiki/File:Julius_Caesar_from_a_Cameo.jpg

Julius Caesar was born into the ancient Jules family, said to be descended from Rome's mythical ancestor Aeneus. Julius Caesar came of age during the chaotic conflict between Marius and Sulla. Marius was married to Caesar's aunt. When Sulla regained control, one of his targets was Caesar, who had just married Cornelia, the daughter of the former Consul Cinna, one of Sulla's enemies. Sulla ordered the teenage couple to divorce, which Caesar refused to do. He left town in disguise and joined the military.

Cilician pirates kidnapped Caesar while he was abroad, and his family had to pay a ransom for his freedom. He eventually reaped his revenge on the pirates by seizing and crucifying them. In 67 BCE, Pompey systematically eliminated the Cilician pirate threat, which was impeding sea commerce, by capturing and rehabilitating them into farm work in areas with small populations but fertile land.[39] Caesar returned to Rome after Sulla's death and pursued a career in politics. Soon after his young wife Cornelia died, Caesar

---

[39] Plutarch, "The Life of Pompey," *Parallel Lives*, Vol. V.

headed to Hispania as governor.

Caesar was deeply in debt because Sulla had seized his inheritance and his wife's dowry, which compelled him to link up with Crassus. In exchange for Caesar's political support, Crassus assisted Caesar in repaying some of his debt. After completing his term in Hispania with distinction, Caesar ran for consul. But he needed more political clout to win, so he reached out to Pompey. The two worked out a quasi-reconciliation between Crassus and Pompey and formed the First Triumvirate.

The Triumvirate initially worked behind the scenes, using their political influence and financing to promote their political agenda, beginning with getting Caesar elected as consul in 59 BCE. Despite Caesar's heroic promotion of the land bill, he faced fierce opposition, most notably from his co-consul Bibulus. The secret Gang of Three became public knowledge when Caesar advocated for the oppressed lower classes and land redistribution. While facing Bibulus's opposition, Caesar called Pompey up to the speaker's platform.

"Pompey! Do you approve this bill?"

"I certainly do," Pompey replied.

"Will you come to the aid of the people?" Caesar asked.

Pompey bellowed, "I certainly will. If necessary, I will provide swords and shields."

Pompey's soldiers filled Rome and cleared the Forum of Caesar's opponents. The bill for land redistribution passed, and the now docile Senate quietly approved all of Caesar's bills for the rest of the year.

At the end of Caesar's consulship, the Senate appointed him as Gaul's new governor, and in 55 BCE, Pompey and Crassus once again served as co-consuls. At the end of that year, Pompey became Hispania's governor, and Crassus finally got his wish to command. However, he died in the Battle of Carrhae in present-day Turkey, and his severed head was used as a prop in Parthian performances. The relationship between Caesar and Pompey had already become strained when Caesar's daughter and Pompey's beloved wife Julia died in childbirth. After Crassus died in 53 BCE, the Triumvirate fell apart. Rome's power would ultimately go to one of the two survivors.

After eight years of stellar military conquests in Gaul, Caesar was powerful and renowned, with an army in peak condition. He was also rich, having paid off his debts and building wealth through war booty. His old friend Pompey was now a bitter rival for power. During Caesar's absence, Rome's political scene dissolved into chaos. Plutarch said bribery was so shameless that corrupt politicians publicly counted out bribe money. He said decisions weren't made by voting but by the force of weapons in the Forum, with blood staining the floor. Rome was like a ship adrift at sea, and the citizens began to think their only salvation was a return to a monarchy. Many thought Pompey was an excellent candidate.[10]

Caesar was returning to Rome from Gaul, but the Senate insisted that he disband his legions, which was customary for commanders returning from military campaigns. Marching toward Rome with an army could be considered an act of war against the city. But Caesar daringly crossed the Rubicon River, located between Cisalpine Gaul and Italy, with one legion of five thousand men in 49 BCE. Many senators scampered off to southern Italy, and Pompey fled to Macedonia.

Caesar entered Rome peacefully, politely addressing the senators who remained. He helped himself to the state reserve funds, using it to fund his next exploit: an astounding twenty-seven-day march back over the Alps into Gaul and down to Hispania, where Pompey's army encamped. "I shall fight an army without a leader so I can fight the leader without his army."

Pompey's army was caught off-guard and quickly fell. But Pompey had a network of allies throughout Asia and assembled a new army and a three-hundred-ship navy. Caesar did not have a large enough fleet to take him on, but an overconfident Pompey met him for a land battle in Thessaly, in which Caesar's battle-hardened army routed Pompey's forces. Pompey sailed to Egypt, hoping to find sanctuary, but the Egyptian pharaoh, Ptolemy XIII, had him killed and gave his head to Caesar when he arrived shortly

---

[10] Plutarch, *Fall of the Roman Republic* (London: Penguin Classics, April 25th, 2006), 242-250. Internet Archives:
https://archive.org/stream/FallOfTheRomanRepublicPlutarch.rOpts/Fall%20OfTheRoma nRepublic%20Plutarch.r-opts_djvu.txt.

after.

Caesar wept at the unexpected murder of his one-time friend and co-conspirator and vowed to avenge Pompey. He killed the two men who stabbed Pompey to death and the pharaoh's advisor who had suggested the murder. Caesar was now the last man standing in the Gang of Three, and for the next five years, he would be Rome's dictator. The Roman Republic was gasping its final breaths.

Chapter 11: Causes and Consequences of the Fallen Republic

What led to the fall of the Roman Republic? How did foreign and civil war impact Rome's instability? What role did Caesar play in its downfall? Could it be possible that a lack of war destroyed the republic since revenue slowed down? In this chapter, we will explore what happened in the final few years of the Roman Republic and analyze several factors that contributed to its fall.

Caesar got sidelined in Egypt when he met Cleopatra VII, the sister, wife, and co-pharaoh of thirteen-year-old Ptolemy XIII. Charmed by her beauty and wit, Caesar became her lover and got involved in Egypt's convoluted royal family politics. Cleopatra's brother-husband had forced her off the throne, making himself the sole ruler of Egypt. She left the country, put together her own army, and returned to fight for her throne close to the time Caesar arrived. Caesar got embroiled in the war between the two, and Ptolemy drowned in the conflict. Caesar arranged for a nominal marriage between Cleopatra and her twelve-year-old brother Ptolemy XIV while she was pregnant with Caesar's child. She gave birth to Caesarion in 47 BCE; he was Caesar's only biological son, although some argue that Caesarion was not his son.

From 49 to 44 BCE, Caesar alternated between consul, proconsul, and dictator but was always in control of Rome. Months before his assassination, he was appointed *dictator perpetuo*, or dictator for life. Caesar finally had the time and power to carry out his reforms, such as addressing the unemployment and debt of the plebeian masses and initiating further land reassignments. He modified the calendar and launched extensive construction projects that transformed Rome; he was greatly inspired by the beauty of Alexandria in Egypt.

Despite liking some of his reforms, Rome's senators feared Caesar would turn the republic back into a monarchy and plotted his murder. On March 15th, 44 BCE, just as Caesar walked into the Senate, a mob of senators reportedly stabbed him twenty-three times. Caesar's murderers' hopes to restore the republic to its former glory were dashed when Rome's citizens turned against them and rioted at his funeral. The conspirators escaped to foreign lands.

Octavian (Augustus) became Rome's first emperor, ending the Roman Republic.

Caesar's heir was his eighteen-year-old grand-nephew Octavian, who was not the war hero or canny politician Caesar had been. He was a weak and sickly teenager with an overprotective mother. When news reached Octavian's family of Caesar's assassination, they were in Apollonia (modern-day Albania). The household was in turmoil, fearing the assassins would come after them next, but they knew Caesar's murder must be avenged. His friends advised Octavian to join the army in Macedonia, as the soldiers there were loyal to Caesar and would protect him. But Octavian had no military experience. He decided to head to Rome and find out what the situation was.

When Octavian arrived in Italy, he discovered that Caesar's will had named him Caesar's adoptive son and left him three-fourths of his estate. Caesar's assassins who were still in Rome were promising freedom to Rome's slaves in exchange for protecting them. Hordes of people from the tribes around Italy who had benefited from Caesar's legislation were pouring into Rome and forming an ad hoc army.[ii]

Caesar's well-known general and relative Mark Antony became Rome's next consul. Another leader was Marcus Lepidus, who became *pontifex maximus*, or high priest. When Octavian arrived in Rome, Mark Antony refused to release Caesar's estate to him. Public opinion turned against Antony in favor of Octavian. The Senate assigned Antony the governorship of Macedonia at the end of his consulship, but he demanded Cisalpine Gaul instead, marching north to claim the province. The Senate declared Antony an outlaw and sent Octavian to rein him in, but Antony escaped over the Alps into Transalpine Gaul, where Lepidus was governor.

Octavian returned to Rome to discover the senators were plotting to regain political power and eliminate him, giving Caesar's murderer Brutus command of Rome's legions. But some of the legions had fought under Caesar and refused Brutus's command. Octavian marched to Rome with Caesar's loyal legions, announced himself as the new consul, and tried and convicted Caesar's murderers in absentia.

[ii] Nicolaus of Damascus, *Life of Augustus*, trans. Clayton M. Hall. https://web.archive.org/web/20070714144802/http://www.csun.edu/~hcfll004/nicolaus.html.

Realizing he needed the support of Antony and Lepidus, Octavian formed the Second Triumvirate in 43 BCE, a three-person military dictatorship. They split up the western provinces: Antony became Gaul's governor, Lepidus took Hispania, and Octavian ruled North Africa. The opposition leaders— Pompey's son Sextus and two of Caesar's assassins, Brutus and Cassius—held the eastern provinces.

The Second Triumvirate's first order of business was executing all of Caesar's assassins in Rome and replenishing Rome's nearly empty treasury with their fortunes. Next on the agenda was retaking the eastern Mediterranean. When Antony and Octavian prevailed over Brutus and Cassius, the two assassins committed suicide, leaving only Sextus Pompey, whose fleet was blocking grain from coming into Italy. Octavian negotiated a deal with Sextus, giving him control of some of Rome's territories in exchange for lifting the blockade.

Lepidus got kicked out of the Second Triumvirate when he and Octavian quarreled about control over Sicily. Antony became romantically involved with Caesar's former lover Cleopatra. Then, Octavian discovered Antony's will hidden in the Vestal Virgins' temple, in which Antony declared Cleopatra's son Caesarion as Caesar's biological son and heir. This threatened Octavian's legitimacy as Caesar's heir, which led to Antony's ejection from the Triumvirate in 32 BCE and the Senate declaring war on Cleopatra.

In 31 BCE, Octavian (now called Caesar Augustus) fought the Battle of Actium in the Ionian Sea, conquering Antony and Cleopatra, both of whom fled to Egypt. A year later, Augustus attacked Egypt, and Antony and Cleopatra committed suicide. Augustus killed Caesar's teenage son Caesarion but spared Cleopatra's young children by Antony, giving them to his sister (Antony's widow) to raise. With Antony's death, Caesar Augustus was now the sole ruler of Rome, and the government segued from a republic to an empire.

The contribution of foreign wars to the republic's downfall cannot be underestimated. Foreign conquests stimulated Rome's economy when they were successful, and most of them were. The Second Punic War brought 140,000 gold pieces, 600,000 silver pieces, and over 137,000 pounds of raw silver into Rome. One campaign in Hispania brought in forty thousand pounds of raw silver. The once-austere Romans began buying luxuries like fine jewelry and tapestries. This paradigm shift in values led Cato the Elder to warn, "We have crossed into Greece and Asia, places filled with all the allurements of vice, and we are handling the treasures of kings ... I fear these things will capture us rather than we them."[42]

Most of the spoils of war went to the upper classes, while the conscripted plebeian soldiers came home to overgrown and neglected farmlands. Sometimes the task of restoring the fields was overwhelming, and the patricians grabbed up the plebeians' farms at below-market prices. The patrician farms grew into enormous plantations farmed by enslaved people from abroad. Meanwhile, the landless plebeians had to look for work in the towns and cities.

"The triumph of the Republic was also its tragedy. The very forces that drove the expansion of Rome, and the rewards that expansion brought, led to social, economic, and political crises and plunged the Republic into a descending spiral of civil war. The institutions of Republican government failed under the pressure of maintaining Rome's empire, and sole power finally passed into the hands of Augustus, the first Roman emperor."[43]

Callous abuse by the patricians led to escalating civil wars with the disenfranchised former soldiers and other plebeians. Furthermore, Rome faced the question of citizenship for the rest of Italy. Civil wars also raged between politicians in the quest for ultimate power, such as between Sulla and Marius and later between Pompey and Caesar. The civil wars reduced Rome's male citizens to only 150,000 by the end of Caesar's reign.[44] These multiple issues causing social breakdown crumbled the democratic pillars upon which the republic had been established.

The Romans exploited the fighting skills and tax revenues from the tribes around Italy. About two-thirds of Rome's fighting force during the wars with Carthage were non-Roman Italians. Yet, Rome did not grant these soldiers any spoils of war or plots of land in the

[42] Michael Duncan, *The Storm Before the Storm: The Beginning of the End of the Roman Republic* (New York: PublicAffairs, 2017), 19.

[43] David M. Gwynn, *The Roman Republic: A Very Short Introduction* (Oxford: Oxford University Press, 2012), 1-2.

[44] Plutarch, *Fall of the Roman Republic*, 263.

conquered regions. Furthermore, underlying prejudice kept Rome from extending citizenship to the rest of Italy, which the disgruntled Italian allies felt was their due, considering how much they contributed to defending and expanding the Republic.

Because of unrest, the Senate evicted all non-citizens from Rome in 95 BCE. When the Plebeian Tribune Drusus pushed for land redistribution and citizenship for all Italians, he was assassinated in 91 BCE, leading to the Social War between Rome and the Italian tribes. Marius and Sulla fought together against the rebel tribes (this was before they fell out), killing six thousand and capturing seven thousand. But finally, Rome granted citizenship and voting rights to all of Italy's men, almost doubling the number of male citizens.

Another factor contributing to the collapse of the Roman Republic was the eventual lack of war, leading to a slowdown in revenue. While Rome was conquering and expanding, the massive wealth pouring in created a system of corrupt officials who used their new wealth to bribe their way to greater power. The plebeian masses already had little faith in the senators, and the depraved behavior among the ruling class eroded the remnant of trust that remained. As Rome's foreign conquests grounded to a halt, so did the massive influx of income. Rome now had to raise taxes to support its infrastructure, which increased the population's resentment.

Julius Caesar's lifestyle and mode of governing contributed to the Roman Republic's demise, but his assassination arguably factored in more. After Caesar returned from Gaul and was reelected as consul, his reign grew increasingly autocratic. His passion for becoming king became apparent. His image was stamped on coins, royal diadems appeared on his statues, and Caesar enveloped himself in a purple toga.

The conspirators who stabbed Caesar twenty-three times believed they were preserving the republic but instead plunged Rome into another civil war. The lower and middle classes had lost their champion who had legislated on their behalf, and Caesar's murder left a power vacuum. By this point, political norms had broken down, and the people were so weary of rigged elections that they were ready to welcome an autocrat.

The republic functioned relatively well for its first three centuries, adjusting to new challenges while maintaining political standards. But violence reared its ugly head in 133 BCE when Rome's senators beat Tribune Tiberius Gracchus and his supporters to death with wooden chairs. Fifty years later, the war between Marius and Sulla led to the execution and confiscation of property of political opponents.

Senators began using absurd tactics against proposed legislation they didn't want to be passed. They simply found excuses not to meet for the vote, and there were all sorts of procedural delays. One consul declared every day of the year a religious holiday so no votes could be held. With rampant bribery and violence, the political norms of the republic had irretrievably fractured even before Julius Caesar's assassination. But Octavian, renamed Caesar Augustus, put the final nail in the coffin.

Rome was ready for a change, and Augustus seemed to provide a way forward.

By the time the senators assassinated Caesar, most Romans had no memory of what a functioning republic should look like. All they knew was political dysfunction and violence. Caesar Augustus gallantly stepped into the power vacuum and promised a return to law and order. By this point, most Romans were willing to exchange the democratic ideals of the republic, which had not been in operation anyway, for an emperor. Even though elections were no longer "free" and no one could run for office without Augustus's approval, they welcomed the end of the chaos.

The fall of the Roman Republic wasn't due to a single factor but multiple causes. Violent, corrupt, and dysfunctional politics disillusioned the people. The astounding wealth pouring in from conquered countries corrupted the ruling class, who ignored the needs of the despairing working-class citizens. Lethal civil wars tore Rome apart and decimated the population. Caesar's heavy-handed politics dismayed the senators, but his legislation for the downtrodden pleased the masses. Most Romans perceived Augustus as the golden child who would rescue them from anarchy and lead Rome to new heights of civilization.

Chapter 12: Influence and Legacy of the Roman Republic

The shift from a republic to an empire was not as abrupt and complete as it might seem. Rome certainly experienced a shift in senior leadership, but many political and social institutions remained fundamentally unchanged. The complex legacy of the republic continued to influence the Roman Empire through its philosophy, political system, social structure, military organization, and other factors. The Roman Republic was ahead of its time in numerous aspects. It not only influenced the empire that followed it but left its mark on the Western world for two millennia.

One of the most enduring legacies of the republican era was its philosophy. Cicero, Lucretius, Seneca the Younger, and other Roman Republic philosophers promoted political and social ideas that impacted the Roman Empire and the Western world. Although it's easy to dwell on the republic's frailties and failures, it created a fluid constitutional system that accommodated change through the centuries. The Romans found novel ways to address unprecedented challenges as a society, and politics evolved. The Roman Republic had the world's first large-scale constitutional government, which eventually ruled over three continents and endured for centuries into the imperial era.

Cicero championed the republic's traditional political system, and he and like-minded statesmen strove to maintain its principles as the government crumbled. Although Rome borrowed some political ideas from the Greeks, Cicero felt that Rome had shown the Greeks how to do politics properly. He maintained that the Greeks were indebted to the Romans for developing a system that persisted through the centuries and the challenges of unimaginable expansion. The republic's underlying political philosophy was the foundation of its governmental system. Students and politicians studied these earlier philosophical treatises during the imperial age as they coped with the rapidly changing scenarios that rocked the empire.

The word "republic" comes from the Latin phrase *res publica*, meaning "the people's affair" or "the public's property." The Roman Republic was the affair of all the people rather than a single monarch or ruling group of elders. Its distinguishing feature was *libertas*, or freedom, but not unlimited freedom or license to trample on others' rights and freedoms. Cicero wrote, "Law is liberty's foundation, and we are all slaves of the law that we might be free."[45]

The "rule of law" protected liberty by preventing anyone from being above the law. Although not all citizens were socially equal, they were equal in the sense that the law applied to everyone. Cicero believed that a universal and unchanging natural law was intrinsic to human nature. He taught that immoral behavior and false ideology could suppress this innate law. He thought that this natural law was the bedrock of justice. This concept of natural law was reflected in Saint Paul's epistle to the Romans:

"For when Gentiles, who do not have the law, by nature do what the law requires, they are a law to themselves, even though they do not have the law. They show that the work of the law is written on their hearts, while their conscience also bears witness, and their conflicting thoughts accuse or even excuse them."[46]

Consequential elements of the republic's political system persisted into the empire. From its early days, the republic had the tradition of electing a short-term dictator to deal with crises, such as an invasion or a civil war. Once the crisis was over, the dictator

---

[45] Cicero, *Pro Cluentio*, http://www.thelatinlibrary.com/cicero/cluentio.shtml.
[46] Rom 2:14-15, English Standard Version.

resigned from his position. But this position opened the door for an emperor when the Senate appointed Julius Caesar "dictator for life" shortly before his assassination.

When Caesar Augustus (Octavian) became Rome's first "emperor," the power shifted from elected representatives to a monarch. Augustus could introduce laws and veto laws introduced by others. He also had to give consent to those running for political offices. This power shift made the political assemblies primarily ceremonial. Nevertheless, Augustus had to tread carefully.

The Romans had overthrown their despotic king five centuries earlier, and their abhorrence of anything resembling a monarchy persisted. The senators killed Julius Caesar because he seemed hellbent on making himself king. Even though Octavian cherished the same ambition, he engineered his ascension to power with great finesse. He was careful to acknowledge the Senate's authority and ostensibly restored its full power.

Octavian outwardly championed the republican traditions and constitution and was diligent not to *call* himself king or emperor. Instead, he humbly accepted the titles the Senate gave him, such as "Princeps" (first or chief of the Senate) and the religious title of "Augustus" (illustrious one). He also called himself "Imperator" (commander) but was careful not to wear a crown or purple toga and not to carry a scepter. Rather than declaring himself Rome's supreme ruler, he astutely gave outward respect to the Senate while quietly appointing new senators who supported him, gradually building his power base.

The Senate survived the leadership change because Augustus needed to legitimize his rule. His authority came from the Senate, and as Rome's leading citizens, the senators influenced the people's perception of their leader. Rome's emperors acquired the position in diverse ways. For example, some were the previous emperors' biological or adopted sons or grandsons. Others snatched the throne with the assistance of the military. But the Senate had to legitimize an emperor's rule, and the emperor had to keep the military's loyalty. Thus, the Senate played a decisive role in kingmaking, as it granted power to the emperor when he started his reign but stripped him of power if he displeased the senators.

Citizenship was an honor that progressively included more groups of people throughout the five centuries of the Roman Republic. At the founding of the republic, all men sixteen and older from the tribes of Rome were citizens. To flaunt their status, Roman citizens wore white togas on formal occasions. Citizenship gave men the right to vote and engage in trade. Eventually, all adult Italian freeborn males could become Roman citizens. Toward the end of the republic, "freedmen" or formerly enslaved people could receive citizenship.

Emperor Claudius extended Roman citizenship to the men of Gaul.
Gary Todd from Xinzheng, China, PDM-owner, via Wikimedia Commons;
https://commons.wikimedia.org/wiki/File:Claudius_as_Jupiter,_1st_C._AD,_Round_Hall_by_Michelangelo_Simonetti,_Vatican_Museum_(48465336326).jpg

Citizenship became even more inclusive during the empire. The Senate initially fought against people from Rome's foreign provinces receiving citizenship. But Emperor Claudius, who ruled from 41 to 54 CE, pushed for extending citizenship to the men of Gaul

(France) and even admitting them into the Senate. The senators combatted this proposal, fearing that the Britons, Gauls, Greeks, and Spaniards would all be wearing togas, but Claudius prevailed. By 212 CE, the Edict of Caracalla granted citizenship to all free males in the Roman provinces.

From its earliest years, the republic experienced ongoing tension between the patrician aristocrats and the plebeian working class. Only fourteen years into the republic, the plebeians staged their first secession, where they went on strike, abandoning the Roman army in the midst of a war with the neighboring Italic tribes. Gradually, over time, the plebeians gained more and more power. By 287 BCE, they enjoyed the same rights and access to political positions that the patricians had. Lines between the patricians and plebeians had blurred by the time the empire began. Yet, there was still a distinct wealthy ruling class, which now included some nouveau-riche plebeians. As always, there were the poorer working classes and enslaved people.

The patriarchal family system also continued into the empire, which meant the men controlled politics and business while women were expected to run the household. Girls and women were under their father's authority, even after they married and started their own families. Their fathers arranged their marriages when they were as young as twelve, and they had little input into who they would marry. Women would lose their children to their husbands in the event of a divorce.

When Rome transitioned from a republic to an empire, Caesar Augustus implemented changes to the army, such as how long a man would serve. As Rome encountered new cultures and enemies, the military developed innovative strategies and troop formations to fight more effectively. The Roman army used its cavalry more often and improved the technology of its siege engines to launch artillery more competently.

The military also gained more political clout in the transition to an empire. In the Roman Republic, military commanders were often the consuls, and military generals who fought with distinction often won the election to the consulship. This close relationship between the military and top political power continued into the empire. However, the army was occasionally responsible for making a favorite general the new emperor. The military and the Praetorian Guard (the emperor's bodyguards) also assassinated some unpopular emperors.

Rome's remarkable road system began in the early republic with the 450 BCE Law of the Twelve Tables, which stipulated roads had to be at least eight Roman feet wide (a Roman foot is estimated to be 11.65 inches). As the Romans conquered the tribes around Italy, they built roads connecting Rome to their new territories. The central government financed the building costs of these arteries, but the provinces they passed through were responsible for maintaining the roads.

When Augustus came to power, he found the road maintenance system inefficient. He took personal charge of it, as did the emperors who followed him. Although merchants and ordinary people used the roads, their primary purpose was military transport. As the republic grew, the Romans built roads in the new provinces outside Italy. That road system increased to nearly seventy-five thousand miles during the empire.

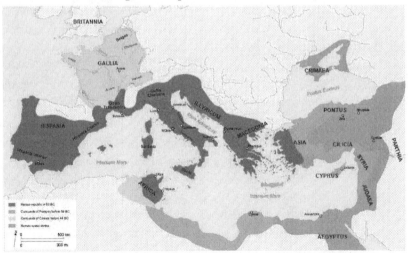

This map depicts Roman territory at the end of the republic.
User:Historicair, Ifly6, CC BY-SA 3.0 <https://creativecommons.org/licenses/by-sa/3.0>, via Wikimedia Commons; https://commons.wikimedia.org/wiki/File:Map_of_the_Ancient_Rome_at_Caesar_time_(w ith_conquests)-en.svg

Over its five centuries, the Roman Republic grew from a modest city-state in central Italy to encompass the Italian Peninsula by 200 BCE. Over the next two hundred years, the republic conquered North Africa's coastal region, most of Hispania (Spain and Portugal), Gaul (France), part of Britain, and Greece. Toward the end of the republic, Rome conquered today's Macedonia, Bulgaria, Albania, Montenegro, Croatia, western Turkey, Syria, Lebanon, and Israel.

This avid quest for conquering territory continued during the Roman Empire. At its peak under Emperor Trajan, the empire contained about one-quarter of the global population. By this time, the Roman Empire included the North African coast, stretching from Egypt to Morocco, all of Spain and France, Belgium, part of Germany, all of England, most of Wales, Switzerland, Austria, the entire Balkan Peninsula, Turkey, Armenia, Iraq, Syria, Lebanon, and Israel.

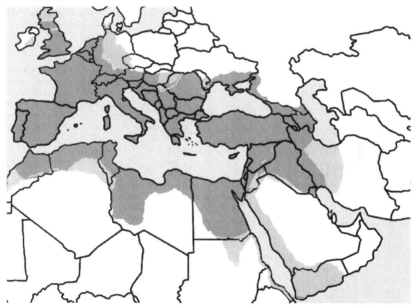

Rome's expansion began in the republic and continued into the imperial era.

As the republic and then the empire grew to cover parts of three continents, it became increasingly diverse, absorbing the religions, art styles, architecture, and other elements of culture. The incredible size of the republic and empire brought inconceivable wealth to Rome. It also brought the burden and cost of maintaining roads, bridges, aqueducts, and other infrastructure across a considerable section of the world.

The Roman Republic was ahead of its time in multiple ways, one of which was its structured government. Rome's political institutions stood the test of time by being flexible enough to adapt to change. Many of today's democratic governments have implemented aspects of the Roman Republic's political system, such as checks and balances, representation of the people, term limits, separate executive and legislative branches, and the veto.

Enlightenment philosophers of the 18th century, such as Montesquieu and Rousseau, proposed that a serious study of politics required an examination of the Roman Republic. Montesquieu's analysis of the Roman Republic's government led him to propose the separation of powers: executive, legislative, and judicial. Rousseau's *The Social Contract* went into great detail on the Roman Republic's institutional workings, which he considered a model of virtue. Rousseau idealized the Roman Republic as a place where absolute power lay with the people, while the republic's administration was the responsibility of an elected government.

Another way the Roman Republic was ahead of its time was by adopting the Forum as a meeting place for government, something that would be replicated for millennia. The Forum was the heart of Rome, the center of commerce, religion, and politics. A vital element of the Forum was the public nature of the Curia, where the Senate met. Government decisions weren't made in a throne room, as with a monarchy, nor were they made by a small group behind closed doors, as with an oligarchy. They were in a public venue where just about anybody could listen in on the proposals, debates, and votes, although only the senators could speak.

The Roman Republic was ahead of its time with progressive technology and brilliant engineering. The construction of its road system, which spanned three continents, involved tunneling through mountains and building high bridges over ravines and rivers. The Pons Fabricius bridge, built across the Tiber River in Rome in 62 BCE, is still in use in its original state, a testament to the extraordinary excellence of Roman engineering. Modern road construction still uses the road-building techniques developed by the Romans.

The Pons Fabricius bridge has stood for over two thousand years.

The Romans had one of the world's first sewage systems, which was built about 2,500 years ago, around the same time as the republic's inception. Although the Mesopotamians had developed primitive aqueducts, the Romans took the technology of running water to new heights. Eleven aqueducts carried water into Rome. The water was held in large holding tanks and then piped throughout the city for drinking, cooking, bathing, and latrines. Public latrines were often connected to the public baths, and the bath water would be flushed through the toilets. The Romans used ingenious technology to construct the aqueducts so the water continued moving by force of gravity as it passed over mountains and deep ravines. When necessary, inverted siphons moved water uphill. They were in a U-shape, so the power of the water running downhill pushed it back up the other side.

The Romans of the republic were genuinely ahead of their time with their political philosophy and governmental institutions, which continued to influence the empire. Their political thought impacted Enlightenment philosophers in the Age of Reason and guided new democratic governments in recent centuries. Their roads, aqueducts, sewers, and military technology continued to be used and developed throughout the empire and beyond.

Conclusion

The Roman Republic's worldview, culture, military, government, legal system, language, and technology left an indelible imprint on the world for the next two millennia. The republic's legacy survived through the imperial era and beyond. It influenced the underlying philosophy of developing Western nations, impacted the literature and art of the Renaissance period, and has affected engineering and architecture to the present day.

The Roman Republic's ongoing struggle for dominance over Carthage and the Hellenistic powers ultimately changed the center of power in North Africa, Europe, and western Asia. But it also changed Rome. Carthage's Phoenician heritage, ship-building, navigational skills, and extensive trade networks left their mark on Rome. Rome appropriated Carthaginian achievements and knowledge, copied their ships, and eventually took over their empire.

Rome likewise assimilated Greek culture and innovations through military interactions, sometimes as allies and other times as conquerors. The combining of cultures led to the Greco-Roman blend of architecture, engineering, literature, medicine, philosophy, politics, religion, and sculpture, which still shapes today's worldview and aesthetics. Greco-Roman writers like Cicero, Plato, Varro, and Virgil influenced Saint Augustine's writings, which laid the foundation of Christian thought. The Renaissance awakened interest in Greco-Roman philosophers like Aristotle, Marcus

Aurelius, and Seneca the Younger, influencing political opinion.

The Roman Republic's internal struggles between the plebeians and patricians and the issues of citizenship and slavery challenged and changed the republic over its five centuries. As Rome conquered much of the known world, the astounding profits of war corrupted its recipients while widening the gap between the aristocratic politicians and the common people. Economic stagnation accompanied a slowdown in expansion, and political infighting gradually descended into corruption, allowing violence to open the door to imperial rule.

As Rome grew from a city-state into an empire, its military inevitably changed. Rather than soldiers fighting for a few months of the year, young men were drafted to spend up to two decades in Rome's foreign provinces. These full-time soldiers were highly disciplined and impeccably trained. The Roman army and navy developed into an unusually advanced fighting force with phenomenal siege engines and strategies. Rome's structured and efficient military led to its unimaginable expansion.

The Romans were prodigious assimilators and replicated some of their military foes' strategies, armor, and weapons. Their war with Carthage compelled them to build their own navy by using a wrecked Phoenician ship as a model. As they honed their naval skills, the Romans proved to be a formidable and almost indomitable marine force against Carthage, which had previously ruled the seas. Rome's naval expertise drove Hannibal to fight Rome in land battles rather than at sea.

When confronted with Rome's intimidating military, many cities and tribes simply surrendered rather than fight a war they'd probably lose with enormous losses. Rome was surprisingly benign toward such cities, states, and tribal confederations. They usually allowed them to keep their own leadership as long as they acknowledged Rome's ultimate authority, paid tribute, and provided men for Rome's military machine. Any state that did not surrender immediately faced Rome's brutal wrath, which could mean completely leveling a city or wiping out most of the population, including women and children.

The Roman military left a remarkable legacy. Often, when one thinks of Rome, the image of a Roman soldier comes to mind, and for good reason. Rome's military discipline, strategies, engineering, and command have been studied and imitated throughout the centuries. Many modern military schools analyze the Roman military and the models of famous generals like Julius Caesar and Pompey.

Throughout history, Rome's legal system served as a foundation for law codes and practices in the Western world. Rome's codified law system began in 450 BCE with the Law of the Twelve Tables inscribed on twelve bronze tablets. In the republic, the citizens' assembly passed laws that were then sent to the Senate for ratification, a model still followed in many democratic governments today. The Roman legal system presumed innocence until proven guilty and held trials by jury.

The Latin language the Romans spoke became the lingua franca (common language) in its territories, which spanned three continents. It gave birth to the Romance languages, such as French, Italian, Portuguese, Romanian, and Spanish. About one-third of English words have Latin roots, and another one-third come from Romance languages descended from Latin. Latin is still used today in medicine, science, and law. The written Roman alphabet, a legacy of the Etruscans, also looks surprisingly similar to our letters today, except the Romans only had capital letters.

The road network of the Roman Republic led to the saying, "All roads lead to Rome." The roads were built so that they traveled in virtually straight lines from Rome to its conquered cities. A few small sections of Roman roads still have their original cobblestones today, and others were repaved into today's highways of Europe. The astonishingly resilient Roman roads used layers of dirt, gravel, brick, and paving stones. A slight decline from the center to the sides drained rainwater off the road. Rome's legions could march about twenty miles a day on these well-built roads.

The Roman Republic was an incredible era in time, as Rome changed both for the better and the worse. It still influences many aspects of our lives, perhaps more than we know. The calendar we use today is based on Julius Caesar's revision in 45 BCE, with a leap year every 4 years adding an extra day to the usual 365 days. His calendar assigned January 1ˢᵗ as the first day of the year. The names of the months we use today are all Roman; they are named after some of the gods, Roman numbers, Roman festivals, and Julius Caesar and Augustus.

The Roman Republic, in all its glory and tumultuous collapse, inspires and cautions us. The Roman Republic instructs us on the factors that make a society flourish and the elements that can quickly plunge it into a disastrous tailspin. When the Romans followed political norms, when they included all citizens in the political process, and when they promoted justice, the republic prospered. When they allowed wealth to corrupt, when they became violent and disorganized, when they ignored the needs of the masses, and when they trampled on political ethics, they descended into chaos. *Caveat lector!* Let the reader beware.

Here's another book by Enthralling History that you might like

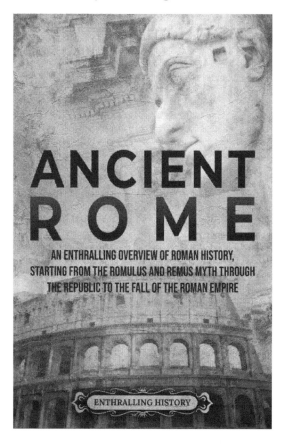

Free limited time bonus

Stop for a moment. We have a free bonus set up for you. The problem is this: we forget 90% of everything that we read after 7 days. Crazy fact, right? Here's the solution: we've created a printable, 1-page pdf summary for this book that you're reading now. All you have to do to get your free pdf summary is to go to the following website: **https://livetolearn.lpages.co/enthrallinghistory/**

Once you do, it will be intuitive. Enjoy, and thank you!

Bibliography

Abbe, Mark B. "Polychromy of Roman Marble Sculpture." In *Heilbrunn Timeline of Art History*. New York: The Metropolitan Museum of Art, 2007. http://www.metmuseum.org/toah/hd/prms/hd_prms.htm.

Appian. *Punic Wars*. http://www.perseus.tufts.edu/hopper/text?doc=Perseus%3Atext%3A1999.01.0230%3Atext%3DPun.%3Achapter%3D16%3Asection%3D111.

Arena, Valentina. "The Roman Republic of Jean-Jacques Rousseau." *History of Political Thought* 37 (2016): 8-31. http://www.jstor.org/stable/26228683.

Barchiesi, Alessandro and Walter Scheidel. *The Oxford Handbook of Roman Studies*. Oxford: Oxford University Press, 2010.

Boatwright, Mary T., Daniel J. Gargola, Noel Lenski, Richard J. A. Talbert. *The Romans: From Village to Empire: A History of Rome from Earliest Times to the End of the Western Empire*. Oxford: Oxford University Press, November 22, 2011.

Bono, P., and C. Boni. "Water Supply of Rome in Antiquity and Today." *Geo* 27, (1996), 126-134. https://doi.org/10.1007/BF01061685.

Bourne, Ella. "The Messianic Prophecy in Vergil's Fourth Eclogue." *The Classical Journal* Vol. 11, No. 7, (April 1916), 390-400. https://www.jstor.org/stable/pdf/3287925.pdf.

Caesar, Julius. *The Gallic Wars*. Translated by W. A. McDevitte and W. S. Bohn. The Internet Classics Archive. http://classics.mit.edu/Caesar/gallic.1.1.html.

Casson, Lionel. *Everyday Life in Ancient Rome*. Baltimore: Johns Hopkins University Press, 1998.

Cicero. *Pro Cluentio.*
http://www.thelatinlibrary.com/cicero/cluentio.shtml.

Davies, Penelope J. E. *Architecture and Politics in Republican Rome.*
Cambridge: Cambridge University Press, 2017.

DiBacco, Cory R. "The Position of Freedmen in Roman Society." *MAD-RUSH Undergraduate Research Conference,* (Spring 2017), JMU
Scholarly Commons.
https://commons.lib.jmu.edu/cgi/viewcontent.cgi?article=1069&context=m
adrush.

Dio, Cassius. *Roman History.* Translated by H. B. Foster. Published in
Vol. I of the Loeb Classical Library edition, New York: Macmillan
Publishers, 1914.
https://penelope.uchicago.edu/Thayer/E/Roman/Texts/Cassius_Dio/1*.ht
ml.

Duncan, Michael. *The Storm Before the Storm: The Beginning of the
End of the Roman Republic.* New York: PublicAffairs, 2017.

Eckstein, A. M. "The Pact Between the Kings, Polybius 15.20.6, and
Polybius' View of the Outbreak of the Second Macedonian War."
Classical Philology 100, no. 3 (2005): 228-42. Accessed July 22, 2021.
doi:10.1086/497859.
https://www.jstor.org/stable/10.1086/497859?seq=1#metadata_info_tab_co
ntents.

Enthralling History. *Ancient Rome: An Enthralling Overview of Roman
History, Starting from the Romulus and Remus Myth through the
Republic to the Fall of the Roman Empire.* Las Vegas, 2021.

Farnsworth Gray, Harold. "Sewerage in Ancient and Mediaeval Times."
Sewage Works Journal Vol.12.5 (1940): 939-46.

Gowers, Emily. "The Anatomy of Rome from Capitol to Cloaca." *The
Journal of Roman Studies* Vol.85 (1995): 23-32.

Gwynn, David M. *The Roman Republic: A Very Short Introduction.*
Oxford: Oxford University Press, 2012.

Hammond, N. G. L. "Which Ptolemy Gave Troops and Stood as
Protector of Pyrrhus' Kingdom?" *Historia: Zeitschrift Für Alte Geschichte*
37, no. 4 (1988): 405–13. http://www.jstor.org/stable/4436071.

Josephus, Flavius. *The Jewish War.*
http://penelope.uchicago.edu/josephus/war-3.html.

Kane, J. Robert. "The Third Punic War: An Intelligence Failure from
Antiquity." *American Intelligence Journal* 36, no. 1 (2019): 161–66.
https://www.jstor.org/stable/27066349.

Lintott, Andrew. "Political History, 146–95 BC." In *The Cambridge Ancient* History, edited by John Crook, Andrew Lintott, and Elizabeth Rawson, 92. Cambridge: Cambridge University Press, 1992.

Lintott, Andrew. *The Constitution of the Roman Republic.* Oxford: Oxford University Press, 2003.

Livius, Titus. *The History of Rome, Volumes I - V.* Translated by George Baker. New York: Peter A. Mesier et al., 10. https://oll.libertyfund.org/title/baker-the-history-of-rome-vol-1.

Martin, Thomas R. *Ancient Rome: From Romulus to Justinian.* New Haven: Yale University Press, September 10, 2013.

Mitchell, Thomas N. "Roman Republicanism: The Underrated Legacy." *Proceedings of the American Philosophical Society* 145, no. 2 (2001): 127–37. http://www.jstor.org/stable/1558267.

Myers, Richard. "Montesquieu on the Causes of Roman Greatness." *History of Political Thought* 16, no. 1 (1995): 37–47. http://www.jstor.org/stable/26215859.

Nicolaus of Damascus. *Life of Augustus.* Translated by Clayton M. Hall. https://web.archive.org/web/20070714144802/http://www.csun.edu/~hcfll004/nicolaus.html.

O'Connell, Robert L. *The Ghosts of Cannae: Hannibal and the Darkest Hour of the Roman Republic.* New York: Random House, 2011.

Osgood, Josiah. "The Pen and the Sword: Writing and Conquest in Caesar's Gaul." *Classical Antiquity* 28, no. 2 (2009): 328–58. https://doi.org/10.1525/ca.2009.28.2.328.

Ovid. *Metamorphoses.* Translated by Sir Samuel Garth, John Dryden, et al. http://classics.mit.edu/Ovid/metam.1.first.html.

Ovid. *The Art of Love (Ars Amatoria).* Translated by A. S. Kline. Poetry in Translation. https://www.poetryintranslation.com/PITBR/Latin/ArtofLoveBkII.php.

Plutarch. *Fall of the Roman Republic.* London: Penguin Classics, April 25th, 2006. Internet Archives: https://archive.org/stream/FallOfTheRomanRepublicPlutarch.rOpts/Fall%20OfTheRomanRepublic%20Plutarch.r-opts_djvu.txt.

Plutarch. *The Parallel Lives.* Loeb Classical Library edition, 1914. https://penelope.uchicago.edu/Thayer/e/roman/texts/plutarch/lives/home.html.

Polybius. *The Histories.* http://penelope.uchicago.edu/Thayer/E/Roman/Texts/Polybius/home.html.

Price, Sara. "The Roman Republic in Montesquieu and Rousseau." *Western Political Science Association* 2011 Annual Meeting Paper. https://ssrn.com/abstract=1766947.

Sheridan, Paul. "The Sacred Chickens of Rome." *Anecdotes from Antiquity.* November 8th, 2015. http://www.anecdotesfromantiquity.net/the-sacred-chickens-of-rome/.

Storey, Glenn R. "Regionaries-Type Insulae 2: Architectural/Residential Units at Rome." *American Journal of Archaeology* 106, no. 3 (2002): 411–34. https://doi.org/10.2307/4126281.

Virgil. *The Aeneid Book IV.* Translated by A. S. Kline. Poetry in Translation, 2002. https://www.poetryintranslation.com/PITBR/Latin/VirgilAeneidIV.php.

Made in the USA
Coppell, TX
10 January 2024